Corporate Acquisitions and Mergers in Sweden

Corporate Acquisitions and Mergers in Sweden

Henrik Wireklint

White & Case

This book was originally published as a chapter in Corporate Acquisitions and Mergers.

General Editor: Peter Begg

Wolters Kluwer

Published by:
Kluwer Law International B.V.
PO Box 316
2400 AH Alphen aan den Rijn
The Netherlands
E-mail: international-sales@wolterskluwer.com
Website: lrus.wolterskluwer.com

Sold and distributed by:
Wolters Kluwer Legal & Regulatory U.S.
7201 McKinney Circle
Frederick, MD 21704
United States of America
Email: customer.service@wolterskluwer.com

ISBN 978-94-035-3160-1

e-Book: ISBN 978-94-035-3161-8
web-PDF: ISBN 978-94-035-3162-5

Contents

White & Case

White & Case is a truly global law firm with a long-standing presence in Sweden, having opened our Stockholm office in 1983. Our M&A practice is the flagship of our Stockholm office, and our M&A team is one of the most well-regarded and experienced ones in the Nordic market. The team frequently represents multinational companies, private equity firms, financial institutions and other clients in connection with their most important M&A transactions, inducing domestic and cross-border acquisitions and dispositions, joint venture, spin-offs, privatization, private equity funding, leveraged buyouts, recapitalizations. In addition, the team is also highly experienced across a range of industry sectors, and regardless of the industry our client operates in, we have likely been involved in similar transactions before and chances are that we will also have globally leading industry experts that can be deployed whenever necessary.

Given our unmatched capabilities outlined above, it is perhaps not surprising that we have been ranked #1 for *Nordic M&A by deal volume* by Bloomberg both in 2019 and to date in 2020 – a clear demonstration of our clients' trust in our capabilities, even in uncertain times.

Author

Henrik Wireklint advises on general corporate, mergers & acquisitions and employment law. His experience includes advising private equity firms and industrial clients on domestic and cross-border M&A. He is an experienced advisor on mergers & acquisitions with a focus on cross-border transactions. He has extensive experience representing multinational corporations on domestic and international M&A (including acting as deal counsel on transactions not governed by Swedish law), as well as advising private equity firms on stand-alone investments and bolt-on acquisitions. He has been involved in significant transactions across a broad array of business sectors, including FinTech, renewable energy, manufacturing, retail, healthcare and a number of high-tech industries.

White & Case

Advokat AB

Biblioteksgatan 12

SE-114 85 Stockholm

Office email: stockholm.reception@whitecase.com

1 LOCAL ECONOMIC, POLITICAL AND CULTURAL ASPECTS

1.1 Population, Language, Currency

[01] Sweden is the largest country in Northern Europe and the third largest country in the European Union (EU) by size. Sweden shares borders with Norway in the west, Finland in the east and is connected to Denmark in the south by a bridge-tunnel across the Öresund Strait. As one of the Nordic countries, the country shares common cultural and historical heritage with Denmark, Norway, Finland and Iceland. With respect to their legal systems, the Nordic countries have cooperated in the development of unified legislation in several fields.

[02] The country has a population of 10.3 million, with a population density of 25 inhabitants per km^2. Annual population growth in Sweden is 1.0%[1] and is mostly fuelled by immigration. Approximately 87% of the population lives in urban areas. The largest city is the capital, Stockholm, which has a population of approximately 976 000. The Metropolitan Area of Stockholm (Sw. *Storstockholm*), where approximately one-fifth of the country's population resides, is comprised of a number of municipalities such as Stockholm, Huddinge, Södertälje, Nacka, Botkyrka, Haninge, and Solna. The other largest cities include Gothenburg, Malmö and Uppsala.

[03] The official language of Sweden is Swedish, which is also one of the two official languages of Finland. The vast majority of the Swedish population comprises of native Swedish speakers. There are five national minority languages, which are Finnish, Sami, Meänkieli (Torne Valley Finnish), Yiddish and Romani. These languages are protected by the National Minorities and Minority Languages Act (2009:724, as amended). There are also six main categories of Swedish dialects that are spoken in various parts of the country.

[04] Sweden has abundant natural resources, the most important one historically being its forests. The country has developed an extensive forest industry and a number of related industries such as industrial manufacturing. Sweden is also rich in minerals and metals and has a sizable mining industry. Thus, Sweden is the home to many large corporations that manufacture machinery for forestry, mining and paper industries. Over the years, pharmaceutical and transportation industries have become significant industry sectors in Sweden.

[05] Sweden enjoys good infrastructure in terms of both physical transportation and telecommunications. The country is accessible to passengers and cargo through its many ports, airports and rail links as well as through roads from Norway, Finland and Denmark. Despite its northern location, ports and airports operate throughout the year and rarely close due to weather conditions. Travelling

[1] https://www.scb.se/hitta-statistik/sverige-i-siffror/manniskorna-i-sverige/sveriges-befolkning/. Information retrieved 2020-09-15.

inside the country is generally easy and, due to extensive road traffic safety measures advocated by the government, also very safe.

[06] Although Sweden is a member of the Economic and Monetary Union (EMU), it has the Swedish krona (SEK) as its currency. At a nationwide referendum on the adoption of the euro (EUR) that was held in Sweden in 2003, the majority (approximately 56%) voted no to the adoption of the euro.

1.2 Government and Political System

[07] The Kingdom of Sweden is a constitutional monarchy and a parliamentary democracy. Finland was a part of Sweden for over six hundred years until 1809, and Norway was in a union with Sweden from 1814 until the union's peaceful dissolution in 1905.

[08] The Swedish Parliament consists of 349 members in one chamber, who are elected every four years by direct vote. The latest parliamentary election took place in 2018. Currently, Sweden has a two-party coalition minority cabinet, which is headed by Prime Minister Stefan Löfven. The Head of State is chosen according to cognatic succession and has a primarily ceremonial and representative duty. According to the 1974 constitution (1974:152, as amended), the monarch has no political affinity and no formal powers. The current Head of State is the reigning monarch King Carl XVI Gustaf.

[09] Sweden has been a Member State of the United Nations since 1946 and of the EU as well as the World Trade Organization since 1995. The European Parliament currently has twenty Swedish Members of the European Parliament, whose term of office is five years each.

[10] Through its membership and participation in trade alliances and associations as well as in other international bodies both within the EU and worldwide, Sweden is well integrated into the global financial system. Foreign investors do not face any major legislative restrictions when investing in Swedish companies, save for when acquiring significant holdings in the defence industry, in which case additional clearances are required. In general, the country is not protectionist against foreign investors but there are some restrictions. In order to comply with Regulation (EU) 2019/452 of 19 March 2019, which establishes a framework for screening of foreign direct investments into the EU, a new law to strengthen the work against foreign direct investment that threatens Swedish security and public order has been proposed (*see* below paragraph 234). Furthermore, Directive (EU) 2016/1148 of the European Parliament and of the Council of 6 July 2016 concerning measures for a high common level of security of network and information systems across the EU was implemented in Sweden 2018. The regulation entails requirements for information security and incident reporting for providers of services important to the society and certain digital services, within sectors such as energy, transportation, banking, healthcare, delivery and distribution of drinking water, digital infrastructure and internet-based search engines and cloud services.

[11] Sweden consistently ranks among the most politically stable countries in the world and thus offers a secure operational environment for both domestic and foreign businesses. Sweden is also considered to be among the least corrupt countries in the world according to surveys.

1.3 Overview of Legal System

[12] The Swedish legal system is a civil law system. The legislation enacted by the Swedish Parliament forms, as a rule, the basis for all legal decisions in Sweden. The hierarchy of national legislation is as follows:

(i) constitutional laws consisting of: the Instrument of Government (1974:152, as amended), the Act of Succession (1810:0926, as amended), the Freedom of the Press Act (1949:105, as amended), and the Fundamental Law on Freedom of Expression (1991:1469, as amended);
(ii) acts of the Parliament;
(iii) ordinances adopted by the government;
(iv) mandatory provisions issued by Government Agencies; and
(v) general recommendations issued by Government Agencies.

[13] As a civil law country, written law is generally more important than case law. However, case law may have importance when resolving questions that are not expressly addressed by written law.

[14] Legislation is enacted by the Swedish Parliament. The Government of State may issue ordinances pursuant to an act that has been enacted by the Parliament. Most bills are submitted to the Parliament as proposals of the government. Before the proposal is submitted, the bill is drafted by the relevant Ministry with responsibility for the subject matter in question. The Parliament passes, rejects or amends the bill. Ordinary acts are passed if they are backed by a majority of Members of the Parliament. Amendments to the Constitution require two parliamentary decisions of identical wording with a general election between the decisions. This procedure is designed to ensure that the Parliament does not make any hasty decisions that can limit people's freedoms and rights. Current, up-to-date legislation in Swedish is available online at the database of the Parliament at www.riksdagen.se/en/documents-and-laws/. The service is free of charge.

[15] In addition to written law, preparatory texts relating to national legislation are considered a source of law, and in particular the proposals of the government and other texts produced in the Swedish Parliament, including its various legislative committees. Preparatory legislative works provide information on the legislator's intent and, for that reason, such documents are used in the interpretation of legislation. Of the various court decisions, the most important as sources of law are those of the highest courts, namely the Supreme Court and the Supreme Administrative Court.

[16] International treaties and other international obligations to which Sweden is a signatory are binding sources of law in Sweden. The practices and procedures of

the international bodies, which apply such treaties, also have significance as a source of law. Sweden is a party to all major United Nations and Council of Europe conventions.

[17] As a Member State of the EU since 1 January 1995, Sweden is also bound by the regulations and directives of the EU. EU regulations are directly applicable in all Member States, whereas EU directives generally must be implemented by the Member States in order to become applicable law. Other EU regulatory instruments are also binding on Sweden to the same extent as they are binding upon other Member States. The rulings of the European Court of Justice are also relevant because they are part of the body of EU law. Should there be a conflict between Swedish national legislation and EU legislation, the Swedish courts are under an obligation to give precedence to EU legislation.

[18] Sweden is divided into a number of judicial districts, each with a district court. Civil and criminal cases are heard in district courts as the first judicial instance, including matters involving corporate law. In addition to the district courts, there are two levels of appeal: the regional appellate courts and the Supreme Court. For cases relating, among other things, to disputes between private persons and the authorities there are general administrative courts, administrative courts of appeal and the Supreme Administrative Court. Furthermore, Sweden also has special courts, which determine disputes within special areas: the Labour Court, Patent and Market Courts and Migration Courts. Swedish law also allows for parties to enter into agreements on alternative dispute resolution. Generally, parties to significant commercial agreements choose between arbitration provided by the Arbitration Act (1999:166, as amended) and the Rules of the Arbitration Institute of the Stockholm Chamber of Commerce (the 'SCC'). Also, the rules of international arbitration tribunals are used and enforceable in Sweden.

1.4 Current Economic Aspects

[19] In 2019, the Gross Domestic Product ('GDP') in Sweden was SEK5 021 billion (approximately EUR480 billion). The debt to GDP ratio was 22.1% and gross national income ('GNI') per capita EUR49 459. The average inflation in 2019 was 1.8%.

[20] Due to Sweden's dependence on international trade, the Swedish economy weakened during the global financial crisis 2007–2008 and the European debt crisis at the end of 2009. The economy started to improve again in 2016-2018; however, the COVID-19 pandemic has had a serious impact on economic growth in Sweden. According to the National Institute of Economic Research ('NIER'), Sweden's GDP has fallen by around 8.3% in the second quarter of 2020 due to COVID-19, which will weigh down on Swedish economy for at least another year.

[21] The State of Sweden has credit ratings from a number of credit rating agencies. Some of these agencies are Fitch Ratings and Moody's, who have both in 2020 affirmed Sweden's long-term debt with the highest credit rating and outlook as stable. According to Fitch Ratings' latest ration action commentary, the stable outlook reflects their view that Sweden has a long track record of sound policymaking, underpinned by strong institutions and very strong governance indicator. Fitch Ratings acknowledges Sweden's high level of domestic savings and sound government balance sheet, which in their opinion provide capacity for Sweden to absorb the COVID-19 pandemic shock. Nevertheless, the forecast by Fitch Ratings is that the Swedish GDP will decrease by 4.0% in 2020 due to the pandemic, and then increase by 3.4% in 2021.

[22] The activity on the Swedish M&A market was also negatively affected by the global financial crisis, followed by the debt crisis in the euro area. The deal activity increased after 2013 and has, during the past few years, been on a relatively high level. However, in 2019 and 2020 the deal activity fell significantly in Sweden. This is likely, at least partially, an effect of the COVID-19 pandemic, which has caused investors over the world to be more hesitant to engage in M&A activity. According to Mergermarket, the global M&A activity has decreased by 26.7% by the end of the third quarter of 2020 compared to the same period in 2019, and the private equity (PE) M&A market has reached a low-level record.[2]

[23] Generally, income per capita in Sweden is among the highest in Western Europe and the country is celebrated for its generous welfare state. The Swedish welfare society, which includes healthcare, education and social security, among others, is funded primarily out of tax revenues.

1.5 Main Industries

[24] Forestry, metallic ores, and hydropower constitute the historical basis for Sweden's industrial economy. Over the years, the automotive industry as well as telecommunication and the information technology industry have grown rapidly and are now considered the largest sectors in Sweden. Sweden is also known for its engineering and electronics industries. Several of the world's most diversified industrial and engineering companies bear Swedish names, such as Volvo, Volvo Cars, Saab Defense and Security, Scania, ABB, Sandvik, SKF, Atlas Copco, SSAB, Skanska, Ericsson, Electrolux and Assa Abloy. Other sectors worth mentioning are financial technology, health and hygiene and retail with successful Swedish companies such as Spotify, Klarna, IKEA, Essity and H&M.

[25] Sweden derives about 45% of its GDP from exports. The main exports include machinery, metal products, transport equipment, pharmaceuticals and wood. The main imports include machinery, transport equipment, mineral fuels including oil, plastics and pharmaceuticals. In 2019, Sweden's most significant export and import partners were Germany, Norway, Denmark, United States and Finland.

[2] Mergermarket, *Global & Regional M&A Report 1Q-3Q20*, 2020. Information retrieved 2020-11-24.

[26] The role of the Swedish state in the economy has decreased consistently in the past decades. The state played an important role in sponsoring economic development during the early years of the country's industrialization, but due to privatization and deregulation measures, this role has diminished. The state continues to own significant stakes in some large Swedish companies, many of which were state-owned companies before they were privatized. The role of the Swedish state in the economy is now focused on improving market efficiency and productivity rather than attempting to control individual companies.

1.6 Cultural Aspects

[27] From a business point of view, Sweden can be accurately described as an open and welcoming place for foreign investment. Sweden is also highly attractive for foreign investors due to its stable political and economic situation as well as a high per capita purchasing power.

[28] Although Sweden is accommodating towards foreign investment, some aspects of the Nordic cultural heritage can be confusing to foreigners wishing to conduct business in the country. Generally, it can be said that the Swedes value tranquillity and avoid unnecessary small talk. Thus, short, to-the-point answers or other communication that can be seen as stand-offish or blunt in some cultures should not be viewed as impolite when communicating with Swedes. The Swedish culture and society is also very egalitarian compared to many other cultures – students call their teachers by their first names and it is not uncommon to see politicians use public transportation. This informality and equality covers most aspects of Swedish life and can be especially confusing to foreigners from countries with more pronounced social structures among different groups.

[29] The Nordic countries are often viewed as places of high taxation, which is sometimes seen as the main hindrance in doing business in the region. The corporate tax rate in Sweden is currently 21.4%, a comparatively low figure in the international context. Generally speaking, doing business in Sweden is relatively free of political and economic risk with many international risk management companies rating the risk as negligible or low. Currently, the main risks involved in doing business in Sweden are perhaps those related to the labour market. High costs of labour and restrictive laws as well as a highly organized labour force are some of the main issues that investors should be aware of.

[30] The business etiquette in Sweden is characterized by placing a high value on clear communication and punctuality. A 'yes' means yes and 'no' means no in the country. This combined with a culture which admires modesty can often lead to Swedes under promising and over-delivering on tasks. Gift giving is uncommon in business meetings, but small gifts may be exchanged after successful negotiations. The monetary value of such gifts should, however, be relatively low.

[31] Sweden invests heavily in education. In 2019, 83% of adults aged 25–64 had earned the equivalent of a high school degree and 43% held a tertiary degree. The school system in Sweden provides relatively equal access to high-quality education without tuition fees. Also, as a result of the high-performing education system, English is widely spoken.

[32] In 2019, 68% of people aged 15–64 in Sweden have a paid job, whereof approximately 70% are men and 66% women. In October 2020, the unemployment rate was 8.8%, which is an increase of 1.7 percentage points in comparison with the same period last year. This rapid increase is mainly due to the labour market being affected by the COVID-19 pandemic.

2 REGULATORY FRAMEWORK

2.1 Overview of Swedish Corporate Law

2.1.1 Laws, Regulations, Guidelines

[33] The primary source of corporate law in Sweden is the Companies Act (2005:551, as amended), which governs companies limited by shares. Business carried out by partnership, whether limited or unlimited, is governed by the Partnership and Non-registered Partnership Act (1980:1102, as amended).

[34] Other relevant legislation include the Sales of Goods Act (1990:931, as amended), the Securities Market Act (2007:528, as amended), the Financial Instruments Trading Act (1991:980, as amended), the Stock Market (Takeover Bids) Act (2006:451, as amended) and Contracts Act (1915:218, as amended). In addition, certain general principles of contract law such as the principles of freedom of contract, duty of loyalty and *pacta sunt servanda* are also applicable.

[35] Swedish contract law does not deviate in any material aspect from that of any other civil law system within the EU, with the German legal system having had the strongest historic influence on the Swedish civil law system.

[36] Choice of law, jurisdiction and arbitration clauses are allowed under Swedish law and are binding between the parties. Council Regulation (EC) No. 44/2001 ('Brussels I') is applicable in Sweden and sets the rules regarding the determination of jurisdiction in cases involving multiple Member States.

2.1.2 Different Forms of Trade or Business

[37] The main options to carry on business in Sweden are: (i) as a sole proprietor (sole trader or sole practitioner) (Sw. *enskild näringsverksamhet*), or (ii) through a specific organization which may be incorporated (i.e., a legal person) or unincorporated (i.e., an organization, which is not considered a legal person).

[38] Incorporated businesses may be further divided into two main groups: (i) companies (Sw. *företag*), or (ii) cooperative societies (Sw. *kooperativ*).

[39] Companies themselves may be further classified according to the following three categories:

(i) general partnerships (Sw. *handelsbolag*);
(ii) limited partnerships (Sw. *kommanditbolag*);
(iii) limited liability companies (Sw. *aktiebolag*), which may conduct business either as a public limited liability company (Sw. *publikt aktiebolag*) or as a private limited liability company (Sw. *privat aktiebolag*); and
(iv) European companies (abbreviated as SE for Societas Europea) (Sw. *Europabolag*), which have a legal structure similar to a public limited company and formed in accordance with the Member State's regulations in which the company has its registered office.

[40] These companies are seen as separate legal entities or legal persons. Among these, limited liability companies are the most widely used corporate vehicle in Sweden. When it comes to 'hybrids' these have not been given any serious official consideration as to whether they should be regulated separately in the law. However, there is no prohibition on collaboration and especially large companies often organize some activities jointly through a legal person (equity joint ventures) or on a mere contractual basis (contractual joint ventures).

[41] A foreign company may also operate in Sweden without registering a company under Swedish company law by establishing a so-called branch office. An establishment of a branch office is subject to registration with the Swedish Companies Registration Office (Sw. *Bolagsverket*) in the same manner as the establishment of other Swedish business entities. A branch office is, however, not a separate legal entity but acts for its parent company. Furthermore, a foreign company registered within the European Economic Area (the 'EEA') may temporarily offer services pursuant to the Service Directive (Directive 2006/123/EC of the European Parliament and of the Council of 12 December 2006 on services in the internal market) without establishing a branch office.

2.1.3 Limited Liability Company

Purchase of a Shelf Company

[42] The fastest and probably the most common way of setting up a limited liability company in Sweden is to purchase a shelf company (Sw. *lagerbolag*). There are several shelf company providers in Sweden and the most commonly used by law firms is Bolagsrätt Sundsvall AB. Purchasing a shelf company means that many of the registration procedures with the Swedish Companies Registration Office with regard to the formation have already been completed. A shelf company is an already existing company in which no business has been conducted. However, the company still has to register a new name, board of directors, etc. This alternative may be appropriate if a foreign company would like to optimize the timeline as the shelf company may initiate its business the same day the purchase is completed and a written notification of the newly appointed members of the board of directors is submitted to the Swedish Companies Registration Office.

General Principles of Limited Liability Companies

[43] General principles of limited liability companies are enacted mainly in the first to fourth chapter of the Companies Act. These general principles form the basis of the whole Act and must be used in the interpretation of the Act. The principles are, *inter alia*:

(i) legal personality and the limited liability of shareholders;
(ii) capital and its stability;
(iii) the transferability of shares;
(iv) the profit-generating purpose of a limited liability company; and
(v) the principle of equal treatment.

[44] The most important principles from a corporate governance point of view are the purpose of a limited liability company, the principle of equal treatment of shareholders and the management's duty of care. The purpose of a limited liability company is to generate profits for its shareholders, unless otherwise provided in the articles of association. According to the principle of equal treatment, all shares shall carry the same rights in the company unless otherwise provided in the articles of association. Furthermore, no decisions can be made or other measures taken that unjustly benefit a shareholder or another person at the expense of the company or another shareholder.

[45] Pursuant to the Companies Act, the management of a company has an obligation to act carefully (duty of care) and promote the best interests of the company. The obligation to promote the best interests of the company usually corresponds to promoting the business of the company and, indirectly, the interests of the shareholders as a group. In addition to these obligations, the management must seek to ensure the equal treatment of all shares, and each member of the board of directors must comply with the conflict of interest provisions (duty of loyalty).

Public and Private Limited Liability Companies

[46] Under the Companies Act, limited liability companies can be either public or private companies. The main difference between public and private companies is that only the securities of a public company may be admitted to public trading, governed by the Securities Market Act. Also, certain provisions in the Companies Act are only applicable to public companies.

[47] A limited liability company can be established by one or more founding shareholders, who can be either legal entities or private individuals, upon the execution of a written memorandum of association, signed by all founding shareholders. By signing the memorandum of association, a shareholder subscribes for such quantity of shares as indicated in the memorandum of association.

[48] The minimum contents of the memorandum of association include:

(i) the date of entry into the memorandum of association;
(ii) the quantity of shares subscribed for by each of the shareholders;
(iii) the subscription price; and

(iv) the names and personal identification numbers of all members of the board of directors and, where applicable, auditors, alternate members of the board of directors, alternate auditors and general examiners.

[49] The company's articles of association must be attached to the memorandum of association. The minimum contents of the articles of association include:

(i) the company's trade name;
(ii) the location in Sweden in which the company has its registered office;
(iii) the company's field(s) of operation;
(iv) the share capital or, where applicable, the minimum and maximum share capital;
(v) the number of shares or, where applicable, the minimum and maximum number of shares;
(vi) the number, or the minimum and maximum number, of members of the board of directors;
(vii) the number, or the minimum and maximum number, of alternate directors, where such shall be appointed;
(viii) the number, or the minimum and maximum number, of auditors, where an auditor shall be appointed pursuant to the Companies Act;
(ix) the procedure for convening general meetings; and
(x) the period of time to be covered by the company's financial year.

[50] As a general principle, all shares have equal rights in the company. However, a company may state in its articles of association that the company has or can have different classes of shares with different rights or obligations. Shares belong to different classes when they: (i) differ from each other as regards to voting rights or rights in relation to the distribution of the assets of the company, or (ii) are otherwise designated in the articles of association as belonging to different classes. The minimum share capital of a private company is SEK25 000 and that of a public company is SEK500 000. It is not permitted to issue shares with greater voting rights difference than 1 to 10. As a rule, the subscription price of a share is to be credited to the share capital, unless it is otherwise provided in the memorandum of association, the articles of association or in the Accounting Act (1999:1078, as amended).

[51] A subscription price paid in cash is to be deposited on a separate account opened by the founding shareholder for such purpose at a bank, credit-market undertaking or equivalent foreign credit institution in a state within the EEA. If the subscription price is paid in full or in part with other assets (contribution in kind), the assets must at the time of conveyance have financial value to the company at least equal to the price thus paid. An undertaking to perform work or services may not be used as contribution in kind. Any provisions on the payment of the subscription price in kind must be included in the memorandum of association. The company may only be registered with the Swedish Companies Registration Office if the subscription price, whether in cash or in kind, has been fully paid at that time.

[52] Shareholders' agreements are commonly used instruments which enable contractual arrangements regarding certain matters agreed upon by shareholders of a limited liability company. Excluding the non-dispositive matters provided for in the Companies Act, the shareholders are free to agree upon any other matters concerning the limited liability company as they wish. A shareholders' agreement would typically govern such dispositive matters. A breach of a shareholders' agreement has consequences in contract law among the parties, such as an obligation to pay contractual damages, but not under corporate law, which is assessed independently. A shareholders' agreement would bind only the parties to it and, consequently, it could not be relied upon in claims against any third parties, the company itself included, unless the company is also party to the shareholders' agreement.

Registration with the Swedish Companies Registration Office

[53] A limited liability company becomes fully incorporated upon registration with the Swedish Companies Register, which forms part of the Swedish Companies Registration Office. The company must notify the Swedish Companies Registration Office for registration within six months of the signing of the memorandum of association, failure of which the incorporation would lapse. The company is incorporated on the date on which it is registered with the Swedish Companies Registration Office. Documents and forms submitted to the Swedish Companies Registration Office must be in Swedish.

Tax Registration

[54] A limited liability company must also be registered with the Swedish Tax Agency (Sw. *Skatteverket*). Filing such start-up notification with the Swedish Tax Agency will result in the company's entry into the register of value added tax (VAT) liable businesses, of employers or persons liable for paying tax on insurance premiums or the prepayment register of taxpayers. However, the obligation to register depends on the nature of the business operation. For example, a company may not need to become VAT registered if the company is not deemed to have a permanent establishment in Sweden.

Financial Reporting Requirements

[55] Swedish corporate law includes extensive reporting requirements for limited liability companies. All such companies are subject to an accounting obligation and must prepare annual accounts at the end of each financial year and file them with the Swedish Companies Registration Office within seven months of the end of each financial year.

[56] In addition to the annual accounts, which include key performance figures of the company, such as the income statement, an annual report must also be submitted to the Swedish Companies Registration Office. The requirements for the annual documents are listed in the Annual Reports Act (1995:1554, as amended), which follows standards set by EU legislation. It is also mandatory for listed companies to apply the International Financial Reporting Standards ('IFRS').

[57] The Companies Act also contains provisions on public notices a company must send in the event of changes affecting the company. Generally, a public notice must be sent to the creditors of the company in the event of a merger, demerger or reduction of share capital. Public notices serve as an invitation for creditors to be heard on issues regarding their outstanding accounts receivables.

[58] The Securities Market Act and the Financial Instruments Trading Act contain disclosure obligations regarding securities issued by listed companies. The disclosure obligations are divided into information that must be disclosed either periodically or on an ongoing basis. Information regarding the issuer's financial reporting must be released periodically. The ongoing disclosure obligation includes information that could materially affect the value of the company's shares. The details of the ongoing disclosure obligation are included in Regulation (EU) No. 596/2014 of the European Parliament and of the Council on market abuse (the 'Market Abuse Regulation').

Corporate Structure

General Meeting

[59] The shareholders exercise their decision-making power at the general meeting. The ordinary general meeting must be held within six months of the end of each financial year.

[60] Pursuant to the Companies Act, the following decisions must be made at the ordinary general meeting:

(i) adoption of the financial statements, which in a parent company means also the adoption of the consolidated financial statements;
(ii) use of the profit shown on the balance sheet;
(iii) whether to discharge the members of the board of directors and the managing director from liability;
(iv) election of the members of the board of directors and the auditor, unless it is otherwise provided in the Companies Act or in the company's articles of association on their term or election; and
(v) other matters that according to the company's articles of association are to be decided by the ordinary general meeting.

[61] An extraordinary general meeting can be held as and when necessary. However, an extraordinary general meeting must be held in the following circumstances:

(i) when the board of directors considers it necessary;
(ii) when an auditor demands an extraordinary meeting to be convened to address a specified matter; or
(iii) when owners of not less than one-tenth of all shares in the company demand the same.

[62] When an actual meeting is held, a proposal that has been supported by more than half of the votes cast shall constitute a decision of the general meeting, unless otherwise provided in the Companies Act.

[63] However, a unanimous vote of shareholders may make a decision without holding a meeting (*per capsulam*) in a matter within the competence of the general meeting. The decision must be written and signed. If the company has more than one shareholder, at least two of them must sign the decision. In other respects, the provisions on the minutes of the general meeting apply to such written decision.

[64] If a decision must be made by qualified majority, a proposal that has been supported by at least two-thirds of the votes cast and the shares represented at the meeting shall constitute a decision.

[65] Unless it is otherwise provided for in the Companies Act or the articles of association, the following decisions shall be made by qualified majority:

(i) amendments to the articles of association;
(ii) a resolution to derogate from the shareholders' pre-emption rights to issues of option rights and other special rights entitling to shares;
(iii) acquisition of own shares in a public company;
(iv) directed acquisition of own shares;
(v) mergers and demergers; and
(vi) reduction of share capital.

[66] The requirement to have a qualified majority may not be altered or mitigated in the articles of association.

[67] In an election of the members of the board of directors and auditors, the person receiving the most votes is elected. In the event of a tie, an election is decided by drawing lots, unless the general meeting decides prior to the election that a new vote shall be held in the event of a tied vote. The requirement of a majority may be amended by way of the articles of association. The articles of association may not, however, prescribe that a valid election requires more than a relative majority of the votes.

Board of Directors

[68] Pursuant to the Companies Act, a limited liability company must have a board of directors consisting of one or more regular members. The minimum and maximum number of regular members shall be provided in the articles of association. If there are fewer than three members, at least one deputy member must be elected. If there are several members of the board of directors, they must elect a chairman from among them. If all members of the board of directors are residing outside of Sweden a limited liability company must have a representative in Sweden who can accept service on behalf of the company. This representative must be registered in the Swedish population register. At least half of the board members, at least half of the deputy board members, the managing director and all deputy managing directors must reside within the EEA. The requirements concern residency, not citizenship. If a company cannot fulfil the requirements of residence it is possible to apply for an exemption with the Swedish Companies Registration Office; however, it is only granted in extraordinary cases and for a short period of time. Employees of a company have a right to appoint employee representatives as members of the board of directors if: (i) the company is of a certain size (employs on average at least twenty-five employees in Sweden in the most recent financial year) and (ii) a decision is taken by a trade union.

[69] The general meeting elects the members of the board of directors. It may be provided in the articles of association that one or more of the members shall be appointed in another manner. However, the board of directors may not appoint a member of its own board. A member of the board of directors may be dismissed prior to the conclusion of a term by the body who appointed such member.

[70] Pursuant to the Companies Act, the members of the board of directors are under an obligation to act with due care and promote the best interests of the company. The board of directors represents the company and sees to the administration of the company and the appropriate organization of its operations (general competence). The board of directors is responsible for delegating responsibility over the management of the company accounts and finances. The board of directors or its members must not comply with a decision of the general meeting or the board of directors where it is contrary to the Companies Act or the articles of association of the company.

[71] While the board of directors is a mandatory corporate body, it is optional for a private limited liability company to have a managing director. If a managing director is appointed, he or she represents the company in matters falling within the managing director's duties, which include the following:

(i) responsibility over the executive management of the company in accordance with the instructions and orders given by the board of directors (general competence);
(ii) responsibility over the accounts of the company ensuring that they are in compliance with the law and that the company's financial affairs have been arranged in a reliable manner; and
(iii) responsibility over supplying the members of the board of directors with the information necessary for the performance of their duties as directors.

Auditor

[72] The general meeting elects an auditor to examine the company's annual accounts to ensure their authenticity and compliance with the Companies Act and the Annual Reports Act. There is no obligation to elect an auditor for a private company where not more than one of the following conditions was met in both the latest completed financial year and the financial year immediately preceding it:

(i) the balance sheet total exceeds SEK1.5 million;
(ii) the net sales or comparable revenue exceeds SEK3 million; or
(iii) the average number of employees exceeds three.

[73] An auditor always has to be elected for a parent company of a group where the group fulfils more than one of the conditions set forth above and for companies whose principal activities consist of holding and managing securities. At least one of the auditors elected by the general meeting has to be authorized according to the Public Accountants Act (2001:883, as amended) if the company's securities are traded on a stock exchange or if at least two of the following conditions were met in both the latest completed financial year and the financial year immediately preceding it:

(i) the balance sheet total exceeds SEK40 million;
(ii) the net sales or comparable revenue exceeds SEK80 million; or
(iii) the average number of employees exceeds fifty.

Management's Liability

[74] Members of the board of directors and the managing director are liable for the loss that they, in violation of the management's duty of care, have deliberately or negligently caused to the company. Such persons are likewise liable for the loss that they, in violation of other provisions of the Companies Act, the articles of association or applicable annual reports legislation, have deliberately or negligently caused to a shareholder or a third party.

Shareholders

[75] A limited liability company is a legal person distinct from its shareholders. As a main rule, with very limited exceptions, the shareholders have no personal liability for the obligations of the company.

[76] The shareholders are obliged to pay the subscription price of the subscribed shares. The board of directors may declare the right to a share forfeited if the subscription price has not been paid by the due date and the board of directors has not granted an extension to the subscriber.

Authority of Shareholders and Board of Directors

[77] As a general rule, the general meeting of shareholders is authorized to make decisions in matters that have been defined to fall within its scope of authority in the Companies Act and/or the articles of association. Certain matters, as defined in the Companies Act, are solely for the general meeting to decide upon. However, it is possible that pursuant to the articles of association, the general meeting may also be authorized in certain events to decide upon matters that fall within the general competence of the board of directors or the managing director.

[78] Further, the board of directors may refer a matter that would otherwise fall within its general powers or the duties of the managing director to the attention of the general meeting. This does not require any explicit provisions in the articles of association.

[79] The general meeting is not obliged to make decisions in matters that fall within the general powers of the board of directors or the managing director if such matters have been delegated to the general meeting by another corporate body, such as the board of directors. In such situation, the liability attached to such decision-making remains with the corporate body that delegated the matter. Nevertheless, the general meeting may not refuse to decide upon matters which have been referred to it in the articles of association.

Representation

[80] Pursuant to the Companies Act, a company can be represented by virtue of position or rank in the company, or by designation. The former applies to the members of the board of directors or the managing director when the articles of association provide them with such representative rights. The latter comes into effect when the board of directors grants this right to a member or members of the board, the managing director or some other designated person, in which case the right to represent the company is personal and not subject to position or rank.

Minority Shareholder Rights

[81] The principle of equal treatment of shares and, in most cases, shareholders is one of the leading principles of the Companies Act. No corporate decision that would grant unjust benefit to a shareholder or other party at the expense of another shareholder can be made at a general meeting or by the board of directors or management of the company. Minority shareholders could object a corporate decision made at a general meeting that violates this principle. Corporate resolutions made by the board of directors or management that violate this principle may subject the directors and/or officers of the company to liability for damages.

General Meeting

[82] An extraordinary general meeting shall be held if an auditor or shareholders with at least 10% of all shares so demand in writing in order for a given matter to be dealt with. Also, a shareholder shall have the right to have a matter falling within the competence of the general meeting dealt with by the general meeting if the shareholder so demands in writing well in advance of the meeting, so that the matter can be mentioned in the notice for the meeting.

Right to Redeem Minority Shares

[83] According to the Companies Act, a majority shareholder with more than 90% of the shares and votes can redeem the shares owned by the minority shareholders. If this threshold is not met, the right to redemption does not exist. Correspondingly, in such circumstances the minority shareholders can demand the majority shareholder to redeem such shares.

[84] The redemption right or obligation can arise not only through directly held shares but also from indirect shareholdings. According to the Companies Act, the shares and voting rights of controlled corporate entities or foundations are taken into account when calculating the 90% threshold.

[85] The redemption right or obligation relates to shares and does not directly apply to any warrants or other special rights granted by the company. However, the terms and conditions of such rights must include provisions on the status of such rights in connection with redemption of minority shareholders. Therefore, it is possible that the terms and conditions of warrants or other special rights stipulate that such instruments must be redeemed simultaneously with shares. In the absence of such provision, the majority shareholder does not have a right or obligation to redeem the warrants and/or other special rights.

[86] Any disputes concerning the redemption right or the redemption price are to be resolved by three arbitrators in accordance with Chapter 22 of the Companies Act. In the case of listed companies, with widespread shareholding commencement of arbitration proceedings, together with the appointment of a trustee to represent passive minority shareholders, is the only practicable way of completing a full redemption of all shares held by minority shareholders. As it may take long time to reach a final decision regarding the purchase price in an arbitration or court proceeding, the Companies Act provides that the arbitrators, or the court, may decide upon advance vesting of title in the majority shareholder. However, an advance vesting of title presupposes that the right of redemption has been legally established (i.e., a holding exceeding 90%) and that the majority shareholder seeking redemption has posted acceptable security (e.g., bank guarantee) for the payment of the redemption price.

Annual Accounts and Right to Demand Appointment of Auditor or Special Audit

[87] According to the Companies Act, decisions of the general meeting regarding approval of the accounts, use of profits and discharge from liability must be postponed to an extraordinary general meeting held at a later date if shareholders that own at least 10% of the shares of the company so demand.

[88] Also according to the Companies Act, if minority shareholders that own at least 10% of the shares in the company or one-third of the shares represented at the general meeting so demand at a general meeting, a minority auditor must be appointed to the company. The minority auditor performs his or her duties jointly with the ordinary auditors and has the same function as well as rights and obligations as these.

[89] In addition, minority shareholders that own at least 10% of the shares of the company or one-third of the shares represented at the general meeting can demand at a general meeting that a special audit of the company is to be conducted by an outside auditor. In such case, a shareholder may apply to the Swedish Companies Registration Office for an order of a special audit of the administration and accounts of the company for a given past period or for given measures or circumstances.

Financial Rights

[90] At least one-half of the profits of the financial period, out of which the amounts not to be distributed under the articles of association have been deducted, must be distributed as dividend if a demand to this effect is made at a general meeting by shareholders that own at least 10% of the shares in the company before the decision on the use of the profits has been made. However, a shareholder may not demand the distribution of profits in excess of the amount that can be distributed in the absence of consent by the creditors.

[91] In addition, other provisions on the minority dividend may be included in the articles of association. The right to the minority dividend may be restricted only by consent of all shareholders.

Litigation and Claims

[92] Shareholders can, in their own name and at their own expense, file claims to nullify any decision of the general meeting or to claim damages from the company's directors, auditors and other shareholders. Even when the general meeting has approved a proposal to discharge the company's management from liability or other proposals not to claim damages from the company's directors, auditors or other shareholders, minority shareholders who own at least 10% of the shares of the company and have voted against such proposal can claim damages from the above persons. The claim can be made on behalf, and at the expense, of the company (derivative claim).

Distribution of Assets

[93] The assets of the company may be distributed to the shareholders only as provided for in the Companies Act by:

- (i) distribution of profits (dividend) and the distribution of assets from reserves of unrestricted equity;
- (ii) reduction of the share capital;
- (iii) acquisition and redemption of own shares; and
- (iv) dissolution and deregistration of the company.

[94] Distribution of assets may not take place where, after the distribution, there is insufficient coverage for the company's restricted equity. The calculation and consideration whether there are sufficient funds available shall be based on the latest audited financial statements. Any material changes in the financial position of the company after the date of the financial statements must be taken into account in the calculation.

[95] Notwithstanding the absence of any impediments pursuant to the paragraph above, the company may distribute assets to shareholders or another party only provided that such distribution is justified when considering:

- (i) the demands that are imposed on the size of the company's equity with regards to the nature, scope and risks associated with the business; and
- (ii) the company's need to strengthen its balance sheet, liquidity and financial position in general.

[96] For a public limited liability company, it may own up to 10% of its shares. The main rule for a private limited liability company is that it cannot own its shares and there are very few and limited exceptions.

Loans from the Company

General

[97] The Companies Act also places certain restrictions on the lending of money from the company to shareholders or others. The loan prohibition targets two types of loans: loans to affiliated persons, and loans for acquisition of shares.

Loans to Affiliated Persons

[98] The first type of loan prohibition targets loans from the company to those closely affiliated to the company, including:

(i) shareholders of the company or another company within the same group;
(ii) the managing director or a member of the board of directors of the company or another company within the same group;
(iii) any person who is married to, cohabits with, or is a sibling or relative in directly ascending or descending relation of, a person referred to in point (i) or (ii);
(iv) any person who is related by marriage to a person referred to in point (i) or (ii) in directly ascending or descending relation or where either person is married to a sibling of the other; or
(v) a legal person over which a person referred to in points (i)–(iv), alone or together with any other person referred to therein, has a controlling influence.

[99] However, the loan prohibition does not apply if the borrower is a municipality, a county council, an association of local authorities or a company within the same group as the lending company. According to the Companies Act, the definition of a group is when a parent company has a controlling influence over its subsidiaries through direct or indirect ownership, has a majority of the voting rights, has the right to appoint and remove more than half of the board members or has a controlling influence through agreement with other shareholders. Group also means any other group of undertakings of corresponding nature in which the parent organization is a Swedish legal person which is obliged to maintain accounts, a corresponding foreign legal person domiciled within the EEA or a municipality, county council or association of local authorities. The loan prohibition applies neither to loans that are intended exclusively for the borrower's business operations and the company provides the loan for purely commercial reasons nor to loans that have been taken up by the Swedish National Debt Office.

[100] The same conditions and exceptions regarding money loans apply to the provision of security for money loans.

Loans for Acquisition of Shares

[101] The second type of loan prohibition prohibits a company from granting an advance, providing loans or providing security for loans in order for the debtor or any person affiliated thereto as referred to in paragraph 98 to acquire shares in the company or in a parent company in the same group. This loan prohibition does not apply when the borrower is an employee of the company or another company in the same group, provided that the advance, loan or security is of lower value and that the offer is directed to at least half of the employees and the offered amount is to be repaid within five years through regular repayments.

Penalties

[102] An intentional or grossly negligent violation of either of the loan prohibitions mentioned above may lead to criminal liability in the form of fines or imprisonment not exceeding one year.

Liquidation

General

[103] In Swedish legal terminology, liquidation may be either in the form of voluntary or involuntary winding up or dissolution of a company. Generally speaking, in both cases the purpose of the liquidation process under the Companies Act is to clarify the financial status of the company, sell the company's remaining assets, pay the company's debts and distribute any excess funds to the shareholders, after which the company is considered dissolved.

General Meeting Resolving upon Liquidation

[104] In terms of voluntary liquidation, the only competent company body to decide upon liquidation is the general meeting. In order for the shareholders to pass a resolution to place the company into liquidation, the resolution must be supported by shareholders that represent more than half of the votes cast in the meeting. In the event of a tie, the casting vote is the one by the chairperson. This quorum may be deviated from in the articles of association.

[105] Involuntary liquidation may take place due to:

(i) a decision by the Swedish Companies Registration Office pursuant to the Companies Act;
(ii) provisions in the articles of association;
(iii) capital deficiency; or
(iv) fraud on the minority.

[106] Depending on the reason for involuntary liquidation, the liquidation is decided upon by the Swedish Companies Registration Office, a court of general jurisdiction or the general meeting of the company.

Involuntary Liquidation Due to Capital Deficiency

[107] The board of directors has a responsibility to ensure that there is sufficient shareholder's equity in the company to protect the creditors' interests. The Companies Act prescribes that the following measures are to be taken in order to ensure that there is sufficient equity to protect the position of creditors:

(i) *Balance sheet for liquidation purposes:* if there are reasons for believing that the shareholders' equity is less than one-half of the registered share capital or if in conjunction with execution pursuant to the Enforcement of Judgment Code (1981:774) it is shown that the company lacks assets for full payment of the enforcement claim, the board of directors shall immediately prepare and cause the company's auditors to examine a balance sheet for liquidation purposes.

(ii) *Initial meeting for liquidation purposes:* if the balance sheet shows that the shareholders' equity is less than one-half of the registered share capital, the board of directors shall, as soon as possible, issue notice to attend a general meeting. The general meeting shall consider whether the company shall enter into liquidation.

(iii) *Second meeting for liquidation purposes:* if the balance sheet, on the date of the general meeting, fails to show that the shareholders' equity amounted to at least the registered share capital and the general meeting has not decided on liquidation, the general meeting shall reconsider the issue of liquidation within eight months. The board of directors shall prepare a new balance sheet for the second meeting for liquidation purposes.

(iv) *Involuntary liquidation orders:* a court of general jurisdiction shall, upon petition by the board of directors, order the company to go into liquidation where:
   (a) a second meeting for liquidation purposes is not held within the given period of time;
   (b) the balance sheet presented at the second meeting for liquidation purposes was not reviewed by the company's auditor; or
   (c) the balance sheet failed to show that, on the date of the second meeting, the shareholders' equity amounted to at least the registered share capital and the general meeting did not decide on liquidation.

[108] The members of the board of directors are jointly and severally liable for such obligations that are incurred by the company from the period when the board of directors has failed to:

(i) prepare and cause the company's auditors to review a balance sheet for liquidation purposes;
(ii) convene an initial meeting for liquidation purposes; or
(iii) petition the court for an order that the company will go into liquidation when the board of directors has such an obligation.

However, any board member who proves that he or she was not negligent shall not incur liability.

Liquidation Process

[109] After a resolution or decision regarding voluntary or involuntary liquidation has been passed, either the Swedish Companies Registration Office or a court of general jurisdiction will elect one or more liquidators to replace the company's board of directors and the managing director.

[110] The liquidator must sell all the assets of the company and pay the company's debts. The liquidator must also apply for public summons directed to all the creditors of the company. The public summons must contain information about all the known creditors of the company. The purpose of the summons is to discover any unknown creditor of the company and must be published no later than six months before the date on which unknown creditors must make a claim. Any unknown claim not presented by the due date will extinguish on the due date.

[111] It is the obligation of the liquidator to ensure that all debts of the company are paid. If the company's liabilities exceed its assets and not all debts can be paid, the liquidator must place the company in bankruptcy. In order to avoid bankruptcy, the liquidator would need to ensure that the company has no outstanding liabilities.

[112] After all the liabilities have been satisfied (or waived) and, if relevant, any remaining funds have been distributed to the shareholders, the liquidator must prepare the final liquidation accounts by preparing a report of the entire liquidation process, including a description of the distribution of the company's excess funds. The report, together with the relevant annexes, must be provided to the company's auditor, who shall within one month thereof issue an auditor's statement concerning the final liquidation accounts and liquidation administration.

[113] After all such steps have been completed, the liquidator shall invite the shareholders to a general meeting for the purpose of examining the final liquidation accounts. The company is considered dissolved after the final liquidation accounts have been presented to the general meeting, as the general meeting is not required to make any decision with regards to the final liquidation accounts. The liquidator must also, without delay, submit the necessary forms to the Swedish Companies Register for registering the company as dissolved.

2.1.4 Private Acquisitions

Share Purchase and Business Transfer

[114] A private acquisition can be made either by a purchase of shares or by a purchase of all or a part of the business of a privately held limited liability company. While in the purchase of shares all the assets and liabilities of the target company will remain with the target company, in the purchase of assets the parties can, in principle, freely decide upon which assets and liabilities will be acquired.

[115] There is no specific legislation applicable to acquisitions of privately held companies in Sweden. In addition to general principles of contract law, the main legislation in this context is found in the Sales of Goods Act, the Companies Act and other corporate laws. However, it should be noted that the Sales of Goods Act is normally deviated from in the agreement.

Due Diligence Review

[116] Prior to any private acquisition, as well as in connection with any M&A transaction, the acquirer normally conducts a due diligence investigation of the target company and its business. Due diligence is an internationally established procedure in business, including in Sweden, which safeguards shareholder interests. The investigation will in particular be concentrated on assessing such risks and liabilities that are not apparent in the financial statements or other publicly available material on the target company. Unlike in Anglo-Saxon law, the acquirer does not automatically carry the risk of not properly investigating the target company in Sweden due to the *caveat emptor* principle. However, the acquirer is often put in a similar position through contract. Except for certain provisions of the Companies Act mainly on mergers and demergers, Swedish legislation contains no direct rules on due diligence.

Controlled Auction

[117] Controlled auction, a sale process involving competitive bidding, is used in over a third of all private M&A sales processes (during the second half of 2018 until the first half of 2019). As the lead times in controlled auctions are frequently short, this places particularly high demands on understanding both the sale process and the transactional law.

Acquisition Agreement

[118] There are generally no requirements under Swedish law as to the form of acquisition agreement, except for certain provisions of the Companies Act on mergers and demergers. Another exception is for transfer of real estate, which requires the agreement to be in writing, to include the purchase sum as well as a declaration by the transferor that the property is transferred to the acquirer. Acquisition agreements typically follow the framework of Anglo-Saxon business culture.

[119] While the provisions of a share purchase agreement always vary depending on the context, a share purchase agreement between Swedish companies typically includes provisions on, *inter alia*:

(i) deviations from the Sales of Goods Act;
(ii) the seller being deemed to not be in breach of any of the warranties made, to the extent that such matter or event is disclosed in the data room that was available for the due diligence process; and
(iii) the seller's limitation on liability, which is usually divided into *de minimis*, basket and cap limitations and limitation periods. *De minimis* limitation refers to the minimum amount of an individual loss due to a breach of the

warranties, while basket limitation refers to the total amount of the aggregate losses due to all breaches of the warranties that must have been reached for the buyer to be entitled to compensation. Cap limitation is the maximum aggregate amount payable due to breaches of warranties. Warranties are normally divided into two categories: fundamental warranties and business warranties. Fundamental warranties relate to the seller's authority, capacity and title but can also include other warranties that the buyer is particularly concerned about, such as environmental warranties. Business warranties relate to the condition of the target company's business, assets, operations, including warranties relating to financial statements, contracts, employees, insurance and litigation. Different cap limitations and limitation periods normally apply to the two categories of warranties. Generally, fundamental warranties are subject to higher limitation of liability in terms of quantum than business warranties.

M&A Insurance

[120] In Sweden, it is common for buyers and sellers to take out insurance for M&A transactions (M&A insurance), especially warranty and indemnity insurance (W&I insurance) for transactions involving a deal value in excess of approximately EUR50 million. W&I insurance provides protection to either the seller or the buyer against breaches of the warranties and indemnities being given by the seller in the sale and purchase agreement. The Nordic markets were among the early adopters of W&I insurance where the PE industry in particular was one of the key driving forces. However, corporate clients are also to an increasing degree using W&I insurance.

[121] The most common set-up is that the seller initiates a process to include a W&I insurance in a transaction, especially if it is a PE-backed seller. But the W&I insurance is only prepared by the seller; the buyer would take out the policy and be identified as the direct beneficiary. This enables the buyer to have direct recourse against the insurer, instead of making a claim against the seller under the sale and purchase agreement.

PE Industry

[122] The PE industry has grown quickly in Sweden in the past decades, making Sweden a leading country when it comes to PE with EQT being the tenth largest PE firm in the world. The companies that PE firms invest in are typically smaller but have a large potential that the PE firm helps exploiting through active ownership and special sector knowledge.

[123] As a result of the rapid growth of the PE industry, PE investments are a major driving force for M&A transactions in Sweden. The buyout market in Sweden is large by comparison to other countries, especially when considering the size of Sweden's economy. Through the last decade, over a thousand Swedish companies have been supported through PE capital, which adds up to around EUR15 billion. This is approximately the same value as the total IPO capital supplied by Nasdaq

Stockholm over the same time period.[3] The largest growth effects have been accomplished in PE-intensive sectors such as ITC, finance and manufacturing.

Financial Assistance and Security Interests

[124] In Sweden, acquisitions are often financed by bank loans provided by either domestic or Nordic banks and, in the case of larger deals, international banks are also often involved. The Companies Act places certain restrictions on financial assistance and forbids limited liability companies from granting an advance, providing loans or providing security for loans in order for the debtor or any natural or legal person affiliated thereto to acquire shares in the company or its parent company. This restriction does not, however, apply as a general rule when the purpose is to acquire shares for employees of the company. Given the restrictions for a target company to provide security for a buyer to acquire shares in the target company, the market practice for taking up securities in the target company are sixty to ninety days after the closing of the transaction.

[125] Swedish law recognizes most types of assets as eligible to be used as security. Generally, assets which: (i) can be individually identified, (ii) have monetary value, and (iii) are freely transferable qualify as security. The Floating Charges Act (2008:990, as amended) contains provisions on the use of floating charges, which are often referred to by the term 'enterprise mortgage' (Sw. *företagshypotek*) in Sweden. Floating charges are available for movable assets only, and a floating charge application must be filed with the Swedish Companies Registration Office in order to be valid. The Enforcement Code (1981:774, as amended) sets the rules on debt arrangements in case of an insolvency. The priority of claims as per the Rights of Priority Act (1970:979, as amended) is as follows: (i) specific rights of priority, which include floating charges; (ii) general rights of priority; and (iii) non-priority claims.

Mergers and Demergers

Mergers

[126] *General*: A legal merger may occur through either absorption or consolidation. A merger through absorption results in the dissolution of the merging company (or merging companies) and the transfer of all of its (or their) assets and liabilities to the surviving (transferee) company. A merger through consolidation takes place when two or more merging companies are united, and dissolved, by the formation of a new company, which takes over their assets and liabilities in return for shares in the new company. In both cases, the assets and liabilities are transferred through a so-called universal succession and the transferee company receives the full legal position of the merging company in respect of transferred assets and liabilities.

[3] Copenhagen Economics on behalf of SVCA, *Swedish Private Equity Market – A Footprint Analysis*, p. 9, 2017. Information retrieved 2020-07-15.

[127] *Merger Consideration:* As a general rule, a merger requires that the shareholders of the merging company receive a merger consideration as compensation for giving up their shareholding in the merging company. The merger consideration may consist of either shares in the transferee company or cash. However, more than half of the total value of the consideration shall consist of shares in the transferee company. As an exception to this rule, no merger consideration needs to be paid in respect of any shares in the merging company if the merging company is owned by the transferee company (parent-subsidiary merger).

[128] *Merger Process*: The merger process is a statutory process set forth in the Companies Act. The merger process (excluding the preparation of the final accounts) generally takes from four to eight months to complete. Also, the preparation of the merger plan may take some time depending on the circumstances of each individual case. A parent-subsidiary merger is usually a faster process that may take three to four months to complete.

[129] The merger process includes the following six main steps.

1. Merger Plan

[130] A merger process is commenced by the board of directors of the merging company, and of the transferee company in the event of absorption, together executing a merger plan. The Companies Act sets forth minimum requirements for the content of the merger plan, and it must include all information that is relevant to the shareholders and creditors of the merging and transferee companies in evaluating the merger. In the event of consolidation, the merger plan constitutes memorandum of association for the newly formed transferee company.

[131] For a merger through absorption, the merger plan must include, *inter alia*:

(i) basic information about each company, such as the company name and number;
(ii) an account of merger consideration to the shareholders of the merging company;
(iii) the date and the other terms and conditions applicable to the provision of the merger consideration;
(iv) the date from which, and the other terms and conditions pursuant to which, the shares provided as merger consideration shall carry rights to dividends in the transferee company;
(v) a proposal for the date for dissolution of the merging company (non-binding);
(vi) an account of the rights of warrant holders, or holders of special rights entitling to shares, of the merging company; and
(vii) fees and other special benefits that, as a consequence of the merger, shall be provided to a director or auditor of either the merging or the transferee company.

[132] For a merger through consolidation, the merger plan must, except for the information stated above, also include:

(i) articles of association for the transferee company; and
(ii) basic information about the members of the board of directors and auditors.

[**133**] After the merger plan has been implemented by the relevant boards of directors, one or more auditors for each merging company and, in the event of absorption, the transferee company must issue a statement on the merger plan prior to its registration. Such auditor shall be an authorized or approved public accountant or a registered accounting firm. In practice, the auditor for this purpose is agreed and appointed in the merger plan. In its statement, the auditor must assess whether accurate and fair information has been presented in the merger plan as a basis for determining the merger consideration and distribution of such consideration. In the event of absorption, the auditor must in particular state whether the merger will jeopardize the claims held by creditors; and in the event of consolidation, whether the total actual value of the merging companies adds up to not less than the share capital of the transferee company.

2. Registration of Merger Plan

[**134**] The merger plan must be registered with the Swedish Companies Registration Office within one month from its execution. In connection with the registration, the Swedish Companies Registration Office will examine whether the merger plan complies with the Companies Act and whether the registration of the merger plan is timely.

3. Approval of Merger

[**135**] The merger plan must be submitted for approval to the general meeting of shareholders of every merging company. In respect of absorption, the agreement must also be presented at the general meeting of the transferee company if so requested by a minority representing 5% or more of the shares in that company. The merger plan must be approved by a majority of shareholders representing two-thirds of the votes cast and of shares represented at the meeting. However, if any of the merging companies is a public company and the transferee company is a private company, the merger plan must be approved by all present shareholders representing at least 90% of all issued shares in regards of the public company.

[**136**] The approval requirements stated above do not apply to mergers where all participating companies are private companies and all shareholders in every company have signed the merger plan.

4. Creditor Hearing Process

[**137**] After the merger plan has entered into force in all participating companies, each participating company must notify their known creditors of its intention to go through with the merger. Nevertheless, the creditors do not have to be notified if the auditors have stated that they do not foresee that the merger will have any implications for the creditors.

5. Execution of Merger Plan

[138] Within one month from the approval of the merger plan the transferee company, in the case of absorption, or the oldest of the merging companies, in the case of consolidation, must apply to the Companies Registration Office for permission to execute the merger plan.

[139] Before the merger takes place, notice must be given to known and unknown creditors through the Swedish Official Gazette (Sw. *Post- och Inrikes Tidningar*). It is possible for the creditors to oppose execution of the merger plan if they file a request with the Swedish Companies Registration Office. The legal implications of not having made an objection are that the creditors are deemed to have accepted the application and are constrained from making objections to the merger in the future. If no objection has been raised, the Swedish Companies Registration Office must give its consent to execute the merger plan. If a creditor opposes execution of the merger plan, the merger plan may only be executed if the opposing creditor receives full payment or satisfactory security for its claim. Otherwise, the district court must reject the application to execute the merger plan.

6. Registration of Merger

[140] After consent has been given to execute the merger plan, the board of directors of the transferee company shall notify the merger for registration in the Swedish Companies Register. Furthermore, the board of directors shall notify, in the event of absorption, the increase of share capital and, in the event of consolidation, who has been appointed as a member of the board of directors and as an auditor.

[141] When the notification of merger has been registered, all assets and liabilities of the merging company are transferred to the transferee company and the shareholders in the merging company become shareholders in the transferee company. This is followed by the merging company being dissolved without a liquidation process. In the event of consolidation, the transferee company is deemed formed.

2.1.5 Cross-Border Mergers

[142] *General*: The 'Cross-Border Merger Directive' (Directive 2005/56/EC of the European Parliament and of the Council of 26 October 2005 on cross-border mergers of limited liability companies, no longer in force) was implemented in the Companies Act in December 2007. The implementation of the Cross-Border Merger Directive enables cross-border mergers of Swedish limited liability companies and foreign entities. Although the Cross-Border Merger Directive has since July 2017 been repealed and replaced with Directive (EU) 2017/1132 of the European Parliament and of the Council of 14 June 2017 relating to certain aspects of company law (codification), this has only been intended as a codification of applicable law and not a material change on cross-border mergers.

[143] *Merger Process*: The discussion below relates solely to the merger process in connection with cross-border mergers where a Swedish limited liability company participates in a merger with a legal entity domiciled in an EEA state other than Sweden, which fulfils the requirements set forth in the Companies Act.

[144] Generally, the merger process in a cross-border merger is the same as in a national merger. There are, however, certain differences in the procedures, relating mainly to the nature of cross-border mergers as involving two or more jurisdictions. For example, in addition to the contents of the merger plan for national mergers, the merger plan for cross-border merger shall also include, *inter alia*:

(i) articles of association for the transferee company;
(ii) clarification on implications of the merger to employment matters; and
(iii) the value of the assets and liabilities that are to be transferred to the transferee company and the considerations that have been made in conjunction with the valuation.

[145] As in a national merger, the merger plan will need to be submitted for registration with the Swedish Companies Registration Office, within a month from the preparation of the merger plan. This registration obligation shall be fulfilled by the Swedish company participating in the cross-border merger. If the merger plan is written in another language than Swedish, the applicant shall submit a translation into the Swedish language.

[146] Also, as in a national merger, execution of the merger plan must be applied for by the Swedish merging company with the Swedish Companies Registration Office, within one month from the approval of the merger plan. As a general rule, permission to execute the merger plan will be granted if there are no opposing creditors (or such creditors have received payment of a sufficient security for their receivables) and if sufficient clarification on employee participation in the transferee company has been delivered to the Swedish Companies Registration Office in accordance with the Companies Act.

[147] After permission to execute the merger plan has been granted, the Swedish Companies Registration Office will issue a pre-merger certificate that demonstrates that the part of the merger procedure which is governed by Swedish law has taken place in the prescribed manner. Such certificate may not be issued where proceedings have been commenced against the general meeting's resolution to approve the merger plan and the case has not been determined. The certificate must be delivered to the applicable registration authority in respect of the transferee company within six months from issuance of the certificate.

[148] The cross-border merger will become effective, and the legal consequences referred to in paragraph 141 shall enter into force, when stipulated by the laws applicable to the transferee company. If the transferee company is domiciled in Sweden, the cross-border merger will become effective when the merger is registered in the Swedish Companies Register. If the registration is intended to take effect on a certain fixed date, it is advisable to contact the Swedish Companies Registration Office in advance to discuss the possibility to implement the merger on such date.

[149] If a Swedish company participates in a cross-border merger and the transferee company is domiciled in a state other than Sweden, the board of directors of the Swedish company shall prepare separate final accounts. The separate final accounts shall cover the period for which an annual report has not been prepared, up until and including the date when the legal consequences of the merger entered into force.

2.1.6 Demergers

[150] *General*: A company can demerge through either a full demerger or a partial demerger. In a full demerger, all assets and liabilities of the demerging company are transferred to two or more receiving (transferee) companies, and the demerging company is dissolved. In a partial demerger, a part of the assets and liabilities of the demerging company is transferred to one or more receiving companies, and the demerging company continues its existence after the completion of the partial demerger.

[151] *Demerger Consideration:* In a demerger, the shareholders of the demerging company receive a demerger consideration as compensation for giving up their shareholding in the demerging company. The demerger consideration may consist of either shares in the transferee company or cash. However, more than half of the total value of the consideration shall consist of shares in the transferee company. As an exception to this rule, no demerger consideration needs to be paid in respect of any shares in the demerging company if the demerging company is owned by the transferee company (parent-subsidiary demerger).

[152] *Demerger Process*: The demerger process is a statutory process set forth in the Companies Act. The demerger process (excluding preparation of the final accounts) generally takes from four to eight months to complete. Also, the preparation of the demerger plan may take some time depending on the circumstances of each individual case.

[153] The demerger process includes the following six main steps.

1. Demerger Plan

[154] A demerger process is commenced by the board of directors of the demerging company and the receiving company or companies together executing a demerger plan. The Companies Act sets forth minimum requirements for the content of the demerger plan and it must include, *inter alia*:

- (i) basic information about each company, such as the company name and number;
- (ii) a description of all assets and liabilities to be transferred to the transferee companies and, in the event of a partial demerger, to be retained by the demerging company;
- (iii) the proposed demerger consideration;
- (iv) the date and the other terms and conditions applicable to the provision of the demerger consideration;

(v) the date from which, and the other terms and conditions pursuant to which, the shares provided as demerger consideration shall carry rights to dividends in the transferee company;
(vi) in the event of a full demerger, a proposal for the date for dissolution of the demerging company (non-binding);
(vii) an account of the rights of warrant holders, or holders of special rights entitling to shares, of the demerging company;
(viii) fees and other special benefits which, as a consequence of the demerger, shall be provided to any person in any matter; and
(ix) the cost of the demerger and its allocation among the participating companies.

[155] If a transferee company is formed in connection with the demerger, the demerger plan must, except for the information stated above, also include:

(i) articles of association for the transferee company; and
(ii) basic information about the members of the board of directors and auditors.

[156] After the relevant boards of directors have implemented the demerger plan, one or more auditors for each participating company must issue a statement on the demerger plan prior to its registration. Such auditor shall be an authorized or approved public accountant or a registered accounting firm. In practice, the auditor for this purpose is agreed and appointed in the demerger plan. In its statement, the auditor must assess whether accurate and fair information has been presented in the demerger plan as a basis for determining the demerger consideration and distribution of such consideration.

2. Registration of Demerger Plan

[157] The demerger plan must be registered with the Swedish Companies Registration Office within one month from its execution. In connection with the registration, the Swedish Companies Registration Office will examine whether the demerger plan complies with the Companies Act and whether the registration of the demerger plan is timely.

3. Approval of Demerger

[158] The demerger plan must be submitted for approval to the general meeting of shareholders of the demerging company. The agreement must also be presented at the general meeting of the transferee companies if so requested by a minority representing 5% or more of the shares in each company. The demerger plan must be approved by a majority of shareholders representing two-thirds of the votes cast and of shares represented at the meeting. However, if the demerging company is a public company and any of the transferee companies is a private company, the demerger plan must be approved by all present shareholders representing at least 90% of all issued shares in regards of the public company.

[159] The approval requirements stated above do not apply to demergers where all participating companies are private companies and all shareholders in every company have signed the demerger plan.

4. Creditor Hearing Process

[160] After the demerger plan has entered into force in all participating companies, each participating company must notify its known creditors of its intention to execute the demerger. Nevertheless, the creditors do not have to be notified if the auditors have stated that they do not foresee that the demerger will have any implications for the creditors.

5. Execution of Demerger Plan

[161] Within one month from the approval of the demerger plan the demerging company must apply to the Companies Registration Office for permission to execute the demerger plan.

[162] Before the demerger takes place, notice must be given to known and unknown creditors through the Swedish Official Gazette. It is possible for the creditors to oppose execution of the demerger plan if they file a request with the Swedish Companies Registration Office. The legal implications of not having made an objection are that the creditors are deemed to have accepted the application and are constrained from making objections to the demerger in the future. If no objection has been raised, the Swedish Companies Registration Office must give its consent to execute the demerger plan. If a creditor opposes execution of the demerger plan, the demerger plan may only be executed if the opposing creditor receives full payment or satisfactory security for its claim. Otherwise, the district court must reject the application to execute the demerger plan.

6. Registration of Demerger

[163] After consent has been given to execute the demerger plan, the board of directors of the transferee companies shall notify the demerger for registration in the Swedish Companies Register. Furthermore, the board of directors shall notify, for companies previously registered in the Swedish Companies Register, the increase of share capital and, for companies newly formed through the demerger, who has been appointed as a member of the board of directors and as an auditor.

[164] When the notification of demerger has been registered, all or a part of the assets and liabilities of the demerging company is transferred to the transferee companies and the shareholders in the demerging company become shareholders in the transferee companies. Moreover, a transferee company which is to be formed through the demerger shall be deemed formed and, in the event of a full demerger, the demerging company is dissolved without a liquidation process.

[165] With regards to the demerging company's liabilities and agreements with third parties, as a general rule, the transferee company replaces the demerging company in the contractual relationship in accordance with the demerger plan.

However, agreements may include specific clauses that could be triggered by a demerger.

2.2 Overview of Securities Market Regulation

2.2.1 Regulatory Framework

General

[166] As in all EU Member States, EU directives and regulations are an integral part of the Swedish regulatory framework in addition to national legislation. The principal national statute governing the Swedish securities market is the Securities Market Act. In addition, the Swedish Financial Supervisory Authority (the 'SFSA', Sw. *Finansinspektionen*) and the Swedish stock exchanges Nasdaq Stockholm AB and Nordic Growth Market NGM AB ('NGM') have issued more detailed regulations pursuant to the Securities Market Act. The SFSA monitors compliance with these regulations. The scope of the SFSA's duties includes various supervisory tasks, including institutional, prudential, market and conduct of business supervision. The SFSA also monitors insider trading.

[167] The Securities Market Act regulates securities operations on a general basis and the operation of the stock exchanges, among other things. The rules regarding public takeover bids are regulated in the Stock Market (Takeover Bids) Act, which is supplemented by rules regarding offer documents in the Financial Instruments Trading Act. The Financial Instruments Trading Act also regulates company and shareholder disclosure requirements. The rules regarding insider trading and other forms of market abuse are included in the Market Abuse Regulation that came into effect on 3 July 2016. In addition to the mentioned statutes, the regulations and guidelines issued by the SFSA and the Takeover Rules issued by Nasdaq Stockholm and Nordic Growth Market (the 'Takeover Code') are important parts of the regulatory framework.

[168] Furthermore, listed companies should operate in compliance with the Corporate Governance Code issued by the Swedish Corporate Governance Board. The self-regulation aims to ensure that listed companies follow uniform and transparent operating principles and rules, in order to promote good corporate governance.

Listing of Securities

[169] According to the Securities Market Act, a stock exchange can admit securities to be listed if there exist conditions for a fair, orderly and efficient trading in the security and, in regard to transferable securities, the security is freely negotiable. Furthermore, the rules of the Nasdaq Stockholm and Nordic Growth market rulebook as well as unofficial translations must be followed. According to these rules, a company applying for a listing of securities is required to provide documentation regarding its establishment, profitability and that there is sufficient demand and supply for the securities, which strengthens the presumption that the price formation for such security is reliable.

[170] The Securities Market Act also prescribes minimum disclosure requirements for Swedish companies applying for listing on a regulated market in Sweden. The issuer must regularly inform the securities exchange about its operations and provide the securities exchange with such information that is needed for the securities exchange to fulfil its obligations pursuant to the Securities Market Act and other regulations. More specified disclosure requirements may be found in the Nasdaq Stockholm and Nordic Growth market rulebook.

Flagging Requirements

[171] A shareholder is required, without undue delay, to notify a Swedish listed company and the SFSA when its voting interest in, or its percentage ownership of, the issued shares in such Swedish listed company reaches, exceeds or falls below 5%, 10%, 15%, 20%, 25%, 30%, 50%, 66.67% (2/3) and 90%. These percentages shall be calculated in accordance with the Financial Instruments Trading Act. The flagging obligation also applies to transactions by Swedish listed companies in respect of their treasury shares.

[172] Pursuant to the Financial Instruments Trading Act, the flagging requirement also concerns financial instruments that entitle its holders to acquire such number of shares in a Swedish listed company, that reaches, exceeds or falls below the applicable threshold, or that would have a similar economic effect with such financial instruments. In addition, the combined amount of existing proportions of: (i) holdings and voting rights pertaining to shares, and (ii) financial instruments may trigger the flagging obligation.

[173] A shareholder is required to submit a flagging notification to the Swedish listed company and the SFSA as soon as possible and no later than three trading days after:

(i) the shareholder has entered into an agreement for the acquisition or transfer of shares; or
(ii) any other relevant change to the shareholding has occurred.

2.2.2 Securities Market

Trading and Settlement on Nasdaq Stockholm

[174] Nasdaq Stockholm is part of Nasdaq, which owns and maintains the Nasdaq stock exchange in New York as well as several other European stock exchanges. The Nasdaq Nordic exchange consists of four local stock exchanges located in Helsinki, Stockholm, Copenhagen and Reykjavik. The four exchanges are separate legal entities in different jurisdictions, but have been subject to harmonization within the major areas of regulation including listing, cash equity trading and trading in derivatives. Companies are presented in segments based on market value and in sectors according to industry affiliation.

[175] Trading in the equities market on Nasdaq Stockholm (as well as for other Nordic and Baltic equities trading) takes place in the INET Nordic Trading Platform. Nasdaq Stockholm applies a two-day settlement cycle (T+2) with regards to all securities. The main trading phases of Nasdaq Stockholm are pre-trading, trading and post-trading. For shares, pre-trading at the prices established during the previous trading day begins at 8:30 a.m. and ends at 8:55 a.m. Regular trading with calls and continuous trading takes place from 9:00 a.m. to 5:25 p.m. Post-trading, during which only contract transactions for shares at the prices established during the trading day can be registered, takes place from 5:30 p.m. to 6:00 p.m. Trades are normally cleared in Euroclear Sweden's automated clearing and settlement system on the second business day after the trade date (T+2).

[176] There are also alternative market places for trading of unlisted shares. Nasdaq First North is an alternative stock exchange for smaller companies in the Nordic countries. Companies listed on First North are subject only to the rules of First North and not the requirements of a regulated market.

Swedish Book-Entry Securities System

[177] It is mandatory for companies whose shares are traded on a stock exchange to use a book-entry securities system, and thus to have their shares registered in a central securities depository ('CSD'). Shares in a Swedish CSD company may be registered in an optional CSD within the EEA.

[178] Euroclear Sweden is the sole CSD in Sweden and offers national clearing, settlement and registration services for securities. Euroclear Sweden maintains a central book-entry register for both equity and debt securities. Individuals' or legal entities' holdings of securities can be registered in two different ways: through an account for owners or an account for nominees. As for the owner accounts, the account holders are seen as the direct owner of the securities registered on the account. Regarding nominee accounts, the securities are held by a nominee on behalf of the custody account holder. A custodial nominee must upon request provide Euroclear Sweden with information on the beneficial owner, such as the identity of the beneficial owner and the number of shares the beneficial owner holds. In addition, securities owned by a foreigner, foreign entity or trust may be deposited in a book-entry account opened in the name of such foreigner, foreign entity or trust, but the holding may be registered in the name of a nominee in the company's register of shareholders.

[179] Euroclear Sweden and the account operators are required to observe strict confidentiality. However, certain information (e.g., the name and address of each account holder) contained in the register of shareholders maintained by Euroclear Sweden must upon request be made available to the public by Euroclear Sweden and the company. As Euroclear Sweden is under the supervision of the SFSA, the SFSA is also entitled to access certain information on the holdings of shares.

Investor Protection Scheme

[180] In accordance with EU resolution, a protection scheme for investors was established in Sweden in 1999. The protection scheme safeguards payment of clear and indisputable claims when an investment company or a credit institution has been declared bankrupt. For valid claims, the state will pay the investor's claim against each investment company or credit institution, up to a maximum of SEK250 000.

[181] The investor protection scheme is available for all investors, whether the investor is an individual or a legal entity. Payment of the compensation is not affected by any debt that the investor has against the investment company or credit institution, which might be a difference compared to certain foreign guarantee schemes. Investment firms and credit institutions are automatically covered by the investor protection scheme if they have permission from the SFSA to perform investment services. The protection scheme does not, however, provide compensation for losses due to decreases in stock value or bad investment decisions.

2.2.3 Public Takeovers

[182] The primary provisions governing public takeovers are: (i) the Stock Market (Takeover Bids) Act, (ii) regulations and guidelines issued by the SFSA, and (iii) the Takeover Code. Takeovers may also fall under specific provisions of merger control under the applicable competition law, or industry-specific advance clearance depending on the target company (such as for banks and insurance companies). In addition, the articles of association of the target company may have an effect on the structure of the public tender offer. The articles of association might include certain provisions on majority requirements or provisions on compulsory acquisition of minority shares, which might have lower thresholds than those in the Stock Market (Takeover Bids) Act.

Tender Offers

Initial Announcement, Notifications, and Financing

[183] As soon as the board of directors (or another competent corporate body) of the bidder has decided to launch a tender offer, such decision must be disclosed in a public announcement by filing a notice of the tender offer with the target company, the SFSA, the Swedish Securities Council and the relevant stock exchange. The offer must also be notified to the representatives of the employees in both the target company and the bidder.

[184] The rules of Nasdaq Stockholm require a listed company to notify Nasdaq Stockholm of a contemplated tender offer where the company is making internal preparations regarding a tender offer for securities of another listed company if it deems that there are reasonable grounds to assume that such preparations will result in the launching of such tender offer. Nasdaq Stockholm must also be notified if a listed company has become aware that a third party is planning to launch a tender offer for its shares. Information supplied to Nasdaq Stockholm is not made public and the exchange uses the information mainly for its trading surveillance activities.

[185] Prior to the announcement of a tender offer, the Takeover Code requires the bidder to secure financing for the tender offer. In addition to securing financing, the Takeover Code also calls for the target company to ensure that other prerequisites necessary for the completion of the bid are present, such as authority approvals relating to financing of the offer.

Due Diligence in Public Takeovers

[186] Due to extensive disclosure obligations set forth in the Takeover Code and in the stock exchange's Issuer Rules, Swedish companies are responsible for disclosing a wide range of information to the market. This includes information that might materially affect the value of a security. Listed companies must also, according to the Annual Reports Act, publish annual financial statements and annual reviews, corporate governance statements, audit reports, financial statement releases as well as interim reports for the first six months of each financial period. In practice, listed companies also publish interim reports for the first three and nine months of each financial period.

[187] In addition to the information disclosed directly by listed companies, a vast array of information about listed companies, such as trade register extracts and articles of association, are also publicly available for a nominal fee from the Swedish Companies Registration Office.

[188] For a listed company to allow a due diligence review, there must be a special reason present. Usually, such reason manifests itself by being in the best interest of the shareholders of the target company. Most takeover bid situations call for a due diligence review; however, the scope and schedule of such review must be separately considered by the board of directors. Individual aspects relating to the situation as well as competition law considerations and the possibility of the bid being completed must be weighed in.

[189] In order for the board of directors of a target company to be able to make a well-founded assessment on a public takeover bid, it should acquire sufficient and appropriate information about the securities possibly offered as consideration and, for this purpose, conduct a due diligence review regarding the bidder, if necessary. The bidder shall allow such a due diligence review to the extent required in each individual case, to allow the board of directors of the target company to reasonably assess the consideration offered.

Tender Offer Document and Timing

[190] The bidder must draw up a tender offer document within four weeks of the bid announcement. The tender offer document must contain substantial and adequate information for the evaluation of the fairness of the tender offer. Before publishing and distributing the tender offer document to the public, the bidder must file the document with the SFSA for approval. The SFSA must decide within ten business days after the filing whether or not the tender offer document should be made public. After obtaining the SFSA's approval, the bidder may publish the tender offer document by filing the document with the target company and with the stock exchange. The target company must notify the offer to the representative of its employees.

[191] The bidder is required to amend or supplement the tender offer document without undue delay prior to the expiry of the offer period if it contains a material misrepresentation or omission. Such amendment or supplement must be submitted for approval to the SFSA before it can be published. According to the Takeover Code, a target shareholder that has accepted the bid must be given at least five days from the publication of the offer document supplement to withdraw its acceptance.

Buyer Exclusivity and Break Fees

[192] The bidder and the target company may enter into contractual arrangements on the execution of a takeover process. The target company may commit to a 'buyer exclusivity', in which the board refrains from actively seeking competing bids. The target company may also commit to a break fee (usually limited to cost reimbursement). However, possible contractual arrangements affecting the takeover process must be in line with the obligations of the board of directors set forth in the Companies Act and the Takeover Code. As such, these arrangements must always be in the best interest of the shareholders of the target company.

Offer Period

[193] The offer period for the tender offer must be at least three weeks (in management buyouts and parent company bids, four) and may not exceed ten weeks. In specific circumstances (such as pending regulatory approvals), the offer period may exceed ten weeks, provided that the business of the target company is not hindered for an unreasonable period of time. The total acceptance period may not exceed three months. However, if the offer is conditional on regulatory approvals being obtained, the total acceptance period may be extended to up to nine months.

[194] Shareholders are entitled to withdraw their acceptances if the bidder has made the bid conditional and has reserved the right to waive such conditions. The shareholders' right of withdrawal may be exercised until the bidder announces that such conditions are fulfilled or until the final day of the acceptance period. If the acceptance period for a bid is prolonged and the bidder still reserves the right to waive any of the conditions that shall apply during the extension, the target shareholders' right to withdraw their acceptances must apply in the same way during the extended acceptance period. If the acceptance period exceeds ten weeks, the target shareholders have, according to the Takeover Rules, the right to withdraw their acceptances from the beginning of the eleventh week.

Statement by the Target Company

[195] The board of directors of the target company must issue a statement regarding the tender offer, which must include an assessment of the tender offer from the viewpoint of the target company and the holders of its securities. The statement must also include an assessment of the strategic plans of the bidder, as presented in the tender offer document, and their likely effects on the operations of the target company and employment in the target company. It is beneficial if the board of director's opinion is announced in sufficient time for it to be included in the offer document; however, the statement must be issued no later than two weeks prior to the expiration of the acceptance period.

Conditional Tender Offers and Amendment of Terms and Conditions

[196] The bidder may make a voluntary tender offer subject to closing conditions. The bidder may also reserve the right to waive such closing conditions. As a main rule, even a conditional tender offer is binding upon the bidder. However, the bidder may withdraw a conditional tender offer if:

(i) the offer is conditional on the bidder acquiring a certain level of acceptance and it is clear that the condition has not been, or cannot be, fulfilled; or
(ii) the bidder has stipulated any other condition for completion of the offer and it is clear that the condition in question has not been, or cannot be, fulfilled and that this is of material significance to the bidder's acquisition of the target company.

If the bidder decides to withdraw a conditional tender offer in accordance with the exceptions mentioned, the bidder is to announce this publicly immediately.

Competing Tender Offer

[197] The Takeover Code does not contain special rules regarding the behaviour of competing bidders. The general principle of respect on the stock market is, however, applicable. As many Swedish companies are effectively controlled by a small block of shareholders, competing tender offers are relatively rare in the Swedish market. Where a recommended offer has been agreed, in principle, with the controlling shareholders, this acts as a substantial disincentive for any competing bidder to interfere with the offer.

[198] In the case of competing tender offers, the bidders should, as far as possible, be given the same information during the due diligence process. This requirement makes some target companies cautious about the level of due diligence they allow a friendly bidder to conduct. The bidder may amend the conditions of a submitted offer, for example due to a competing bid, if the revised conditions are more favourable for the shareholders and at least two weeks of the acceptance period remain after the amendment. However, this does not prevent the bidder from amending the conditions if a reservation for this has been stated in the offer.

[199] The use of traditional defence measures, such as 'poison pills', is relatively uncommon for Swedish companies. Although it is possible to introduce such defence measures to protect the company from bidders, the directors of Swedish listed companies have fiduciary duties that, as in the UK, make this difficult unless such measures can be shown to be in the best interests of the company and its shareholders.

Mandatory Tender Offer Obligation

[200] The Stock Market (Takeover Bids) Act provides that a shareholder who shall come to hold shares representing at least 30% of the total voting rights represented by a listed company's shares must within four weeks thereafter offer to purchase the remaining shares of the company and any share derivatives issued by the company (mandatory bid). The remaining shareholders must be offered cash for their shares; however, consideration in other forms may be offered as an alternative. The mandatory offer may not be subject to completion conditions other than the granting of regulatory approvals.

[201] The mandatory bid obligation will not be triggered if a shareholder attains at least 30% of the voting rights for all shares in the company through a takeover bid which pertains to all shares in the company. The mandatory bid is neither triggered if a shareholder holds shares representing less than 30% of the voting rights, but also holds an option to acquire additional shares which would increase the holding to 30% or more.

[202] The Stock Market (Takeover Bids) Act contains detailed provisions on how a shareholder's holding in a listed company shall be calculated for the purpose of the mandatory bid obligation. In addition to directly held shares, shares held by subsidiaries and other entities controlled by the shareholder are also taken into account as well as shares held together with a third party and shares held by a person who acts in concert with the shareholder in question. Therefore, it is not possible to circumvent the obligation to make a mandatory tender offer through indirect shareholdings.

Disclosure and Timing of Mandatory Tender Offer

[203] When a mandatory bid obligation is triggered, the shareholder in question must immediately make public the extent of the shareholding in the company. The shareholder must also disclose the mandatory bid obligation with a public announcement. The triggering of the obligation must be notified to the target company, the SFSA, Nasdaq Stockholm and the representatives of the employees.

[204] The acceptance period for mandatory offers is to be determined in the same manner as for other offers according to the Takeover Code. As in the case of voluntary offers, the acceptance period may be extended. However, the extension may not delay payment of consideration to shareholders who have already accepted the cash offer and the total acceptance period may not exceed three months, or nine months if the offer is conditional on regulatory approvals being obtained.

Pricing

Pricing Requirements

[205] Generally, the Takeover Code stipulates that any person making a tender offer for publicly traded shares and/or share derivatives may not place the holders of such securities in an unequal position.

[206] In a voluntary tender offer, the offer price may be paid in cash, in securities or in a combination thereof. However, the bidder must offer cash consideration at least as an alternative if the bidder has, during the period commencing six months prior to publishing an offer, directly or indirectly through other than a previous takeover offer, acquired more than 10% of the shares in the target company in exchange for:

(i) cash consideration; or
(ii) consideration in the form of securities and other than through a previous takeover offer for all of the shares in the target company.

In a mandatory tender offer, securities or a combination of cash and securities can only be offered as an alternative to all-cash consideration.

[207] The minimum offer price in: (i) a voluntary tender offer for all shares and share derivatives of the target company and (ii) a mandatory tender offer is the highest price paid by the bidder during the six months preceding the announcement of the voluntary tender offer or the triggering of the obligation to launch a mandatory offer, as applicable.

[208] In a voluntary tender offer, if the bidder has not purchased any shares of the target company during such six-month period, the bidder may freely set the offer price for all shares and share derivatives of the target company. In a mandatory tender offer, if the bidder has not purchased any shares of the target company during such six-month period, the minimum offer price is the volume-weighted average market price for the securities during the twenty trading days preceding the triggering of the mandatory bid obligation.

[209] The Takeover Code does not regulate the pricing of voluntary tender offers that are not made for all shares and share derivatives in the target company (a partial offer). Nevertheless, if the obligation to launch a mandatory tender offer arises as a result of such voluntary partial offer, the above-mentioned provisions on pricing of mandatory tender offers would naturally need to be observed.

Top-Up and Compensation Obligation

[210] The bidder is required to amend the terms and conditions of the tender offer if, after the announcement of the tender offer but before the commencement of payment of the consideration, the bidder purchases equity securities of the target company outside the tender offer at more favourable terms. If a higher price was paid for the securities in the side transaction, the bidder is to pay the balance of the higher price and the offer price to the shareholders of the target company who tendered their securities in the tender offer (top-up obligation).

[211] Furthermore, the bidder is required to pay compensatory cash consideration to the target company's shareholders if the bidder has, within a period of six months after the commencement of payment of the consideration, acquired securities in the target on more favourable terms than of the offer (compensation obligation). However, the bidder is not required to pay the difference between the offered price and any compensation received by the bidder for the sale of such securities afterwards.

Exemptions Granted by the Swedish Securities Council

[212] The Stock Market (Takeover Bids) Act gives the SFSA the right to grant exemptions from the obligations related to tender offers, including the obligation to make a mandatory tender offer. The SFSA has in turn delegated this right to grant exemptions to the Swedish Securities Council, who considers such exemptions on a case-by-case basis. Furthermore, Nasdaq Stockholm and Nordic Growth Market have also delegated the duty to interpret and to grant exemptions from the Takeover Code to the Swedish Securities Council.

Role of the Target Company in Tender Offers

Swedish Corporate Law Principles

[213] Certain Swedish corporate law principles must be taken into account when the target company's board of directors is considering possible actions in connection with a proposed public tender offer or an announcement concerning a public tender offer. Such principles have been set out in the Companies Act and the Takeover Code.

Duties of the Board in Tender Offer Situations

[214] To fulfil its obligations, the board of directors of the target company should take an active role in connection with a potential takeover. The Stock Market (Takeover Bids) Act and the Takeover Code set forth several duties for the board of directors, which include managing the tender offer process in a controlled manner, to provide the board of directors with an opportunity to diligently assess the tender offer and its fairness.

Considering a Tender Offer Proposal

[215] If the board of directors is contacted with a tender offer proposal and considers such contact to be of a serious and credible nature and the offered price (including any premium) is at least potentially attractive, the board of directors should evaluate what measures may be required to secure the interests of the shareholders of the target company. This requires careful evaluation of the tender offer itself as well as other alternatives available.

Possible Cooperation with the Bidder

[216] If the board of directors concludes in its evaluation that the proposed tender offer appears to be the most beneficial alternative available for the shareholders, the board of directors should generally, in accordance with its fiduciary duty, strive to achieve the highest possible price for the securities of the target company. The board of directors should also examine whether the bidder has the prerequisites necessary to complete the tender offer. To secure the highest possible price, the board of directors should, as a rule, act in such a manner that all serious competing bidders have equal opportunity to launch a tender offer for the securities of the target company.

Opposing the Tender Offer

[217] The board of directors may in its evaluation conclude that the (proposed) tender offer is not in the best interest of the shareholders. In such case, the board of directors may be satisfied in only announcing this view in its statement, or it may also seek to take defensive action. Based on the general principles of the Companies Act, the board of directors may undertake defensive measures that have the purpose of preventing the completion of a tender offer only in very exceptional cases. Pursuant to the Stock Market (Takeover Bids) Act, if the board of directors, after having received information on a contemplated tender offer, intends to oppose or take defensive measures against the tender offer, it should typically convene a general meeting of shareholders to consider the planned defensive measures. Such measures may include, among others, sale of core assets of the target company or transactions that deviate from the ordinary course of business of the target company or are otherwise not in accordance with normal market practice. Nevertheless, the use of traditional defence measures, such as 'poison pills', is relatively uncommon in Swedish companies.

Statement Regarding the Tender Offer

[218] The board of directors of the target company must issue a statement regarding the tender offer. The board of directors must provide its statement to the best of its abilities, and such statement must include an assessment of the tender offer from the viewpoint of the target company and its shareholders. In addition, the statement must include an assessment of the strategic plans of the bidder as presented in the tender offer document and their likely effects on the operations of and employment in the target company.

[219] In its statement, the board of directors must take a view on the tender offer and provide guidance to the shareholders of the target company. However, the statement does not necessarily need to include a definitive recommendation to the shareholders to approve or reject the tender offer. If no such recommendation is included in the statement, the board of directors should explain the reasons for not being able to recommend either the approval or rejection of the tender offer.

[220] If the board of directors is not able to evaluate the merits of the tender offer, it must state this in its statement and provide grounds for this view. In addition, if the board of directors has not made a unanimous decision regarding the contents of the statement, this must be set forth in the statement.

[221] It is beneficial if the board of director's opinion is announced in sufficient time for it to be included in the offer document; however, the statement must be issued no later than two weeks prior to the expiration of the acceptance period.

[222] There is no obligation for the board of directors to use external experts in preparing its statement. However, in many cases, to fulfil its duty of care, the board of directors obtains a fairness opinion from a reputable investment bank. Also, due to the rather complex and technical nature of the Swedish takeover rules, it is customary for the board of directors of a target company to seek legal advice in connection with a tender offer.

Competing Tender Offers

[223] If the board of directors of the target company receives a contact of a serious nature from a competing bidder, the board of directors should assess the situation, acquire sufficient and appropriate information on the competing proposal and compare the proposal with the first (proposed) tender offer. To secure the highest possible consideration for the securities of the target company, the board of directors should, as a general rule, act in such a manner that all serious competing bidders have equal opportunity to launch a tender offer for the securities of the target company.

[224] According to the Takeover Code, if the bidder amends the terms and conditions of a submitted offer, for example due to a competing offer, the board of directors of the target company is to announce its opinion regarding the revised offer and the reasons for this opinion. The announcement should be made as soon as possible and no later than one week before the end of the acceptance period.

Possible Post-Takeover Measures

Disclosure Obligations

[225] As soon as possible after the expiry of the acceptance period, the bidder must make public the result of the tender offer, and disclose its resolution to initiate a compulsory acquisition (squeeze-out) proceeding, if applicable. The target company must also, through its website, make public the notification given by the bidder regarding the result of the tender offer. Furthermore, the target company has a continuous duty to disclose all information regarding the company that is likely to have a material effect on the value of the securities of the company.

[226] The Financial Instruments Trading Act provides that target company and the SFSA must be notified when the bidder's shareholdings either: (i) increase to more than 90% of all shares and voting rights or (ii) decrease to 90% or less of all shares and voting rights. The notification has to be submitted in writing as soon as possible and no later than three trading days after the shareholding has changed in the prescribed manner.

[227] Failure to deliver the above notifications to the target company does not have any effect on the redemption right (or obligation) as such, but such failure may result in an obligation to compensate for any damage resulting from the failure to receive notification.

Minority Squeeze-Out

[228] Chapter 22 of the Companies Act provides that a shareholder holding more than 90% of all shares and voting rights of a company has the right to redeem (or squeeze out) the remaining shares of the company from the minority shareholders at a 'fair price'. The 90% shareholder has also an obligation to redeem the shares of any minority shareholder if such minority shareholder demands the redemption of its shares.

[229] In both cases, the redemption price (or squeeze-out price) for shares held by minority shareholders should be determined in such a manner that it corresponds to the price expected upon a sale under normal circumstances, i.e. the market price. However, when the redemption right or obligation arises after a mandatory or a voluntary tender offer that was accepted by shareholders representing more than 90% of the shares that were subject to the tender offer, the redemption price is generally determined by the price in the preceding tender offer or mandatory tender offer.

[230] Irrespective of the above general rule, certain conditions may result in the price offered in the preceding tender offer or mandatory tender offer to be disregarded in determining the 'fair price'. For example, if a relatively long time has passed after the tender offer or mandatory tender offer, or if only a small number of shareholders to whom the offer was directed accepted the preceding tender offer, this could indicate that the price offered might not reflect the 'fair price' for the shares.

Delisting

[231] In accordance with the Securities Market Act, the exchange may, upon application by a listed company, terminate trading in the listed company's securities. Such delisting may not result in any significant damage to investors or to the orderly operation of the securities markets. With regards to delisting of shares in a takeover situation, the Swedish Securities Council has stated that the acquirer should have at least 90% of ownership of the listed company in order for such delisting to be aligned with generally accepted practice in the securities market.[4]

[4] The Swedish Securities Council's statement 2014:33.

Foreign Investment Restrictions

[232] Swedish law does not include any general restrictions concerning foreign ownership. As such, foreign investors wishing to conduct business in Sweden are generally subject to the same rules as local investors and no special permits are required. There are also no restrictions on foreign directors, managers or board members. However, the Companies Act requires at least half of the members of the board of directors to be resident within the EEA. The Swedish Companies Registration Office may grant an exemption to this requirement if any special cause exists.

[233] Even though Sweden has a general openness towards foreign investment, some foreign ownership restrictions may apply to secure the country's national security according to the Military Equipment Act (1992:1300, as amended) and the Protective Security Act (2018:585, as amended). Furthermore, the EU FDI Regulation (Regulation (EU) 2019/452 of 19 March 2019), which establishes a framework for screening of foreign direct investments into the EU, entered into force on 11 April 2019 and will be effective in all Member States including Sweden as of 11 October 2020.

[234] In order to comply with the requirements that the EU FDI Regulation imposes, the Swedish Government has proposed a new Act on Supplementary Provisions to the EU Regulation on Foreign Direct Investment (Sw. *Kompletterande bestämmelser till EU:s förordning om utländska direktinvesteringar*), proposedly effective as of 1 November 2020, to strengthen the work against foreign direct investment that threatens Swedish security and public order. This act will authorize the Inspectorate of Strategic Products (Sw. *Inspektionen för strategiska produkter*) to collect information about certain foreign investors.

[235] Further, advancements towards the introduction of rules that will allow for foreign investments of security-sensitive infrastructure and technologies to be screened and blocked has been proposed to enter into force in 2021.

[236] It should further be noted that the Swedish Government has appointed a Committee of Enquiry to investigate and present a proposal for a general FDI screening mechanism. The deadline for this proposal is the end of 2021. Consequently, any general screening mechanism will likely be introduced in 2022.

Foreign Exchange Control

[237] Shares in Swedish companies may be purchased by non-residents of Sweden without any Swedish exchange controls. Non-residents may also receive dividends without any exchange controls, with the transfer of assets out of Sweden being subject to payment by the company of withholding taxes in the absence of an applicable tax treaty. Shares in a Swedish company may be sold in Sweden by non-residents, and the proceeds of such sale may be transferred out of Sweden in any convertible currency. There are no Swedish exchange control regulations restricting the sale of shares in a Swedish company by non-residents to other non-residents.

2.3 Regulated Industries

2.3.1 Financial Sector

[238] The SFSA is the principal authority responsible for supervising the financial markets and regulatory compliance. Service providers operating in the financial markets must, in most cases, be authorized to provide financial services in Sweden. The SFSA is the principal authority and grants authorization relating to operations in the financial sector in Sweden.

[239] The SFSA grants authorization to, for example, the following entities: (i) banks, (ii) payment service companies, (iii) exchange and clearing houses, (iv) fund companies, (v) funds, (vi) insurance companies, (vii) insurance intermediaries, (viii) building societies, (ix) credit-market companies, (x) electronic money issuers, and (xi) investment firms.

[240] The Banking and Financing Business Act (2004:297, as amended) is the principal act in the banking sector. The Act applies to all banking and financing businesses except for operations conducted by the Central Bank of Sweden and the Swedish National Debt Office. It also sets forth the principles of supervision for credit operations. Moreover, the provisions of the Act apply to operations conducted in Sweden by foreign undertakings, where appropriate. In addition to the Banking and Financing Business Act, there are a number of other specific laws which relate to particular corporate forms of banking, such as the Foreign Branch Offices Act (1992:160, as amended), the Credit Institutions and Securities Companies (Special Supervision) Act (2014:968, as amended) and the Certain Financial Operations (Reporting Duty) Act (1996:1006, as amended).

[241] The operations and supervision of UCITS fund management companies are regulated in the Swedish UCITS Act (2004:46, as amended), whereas the operations and supervision of AIF managers are subject to the Swedish Act on managers of alternative investment funds (2013:561, as amended). The Payment Services Act (2010:751, as amended) regulates the provision of payment services in Sweden.

[242] In addition, companies operating in the financial sector, including but not limited to banks and operators of funds and payment services, are required to comply with the Money Laundering and Terrorist Financing (Prevention) Act (2017:630, as amended). The law prohibits banks and other financial services companies from engaging in money laundering activities and requires such institutions to report to the police transactions suspected of being money laundering. The Swedish anti-money laundering regulation applies to both national and cross-border activities.

[243] In addition to the applicable laws, detailed requirements and provisions relating to the operations of entities in the financial sector are set out in the government ordinances and regulations of the SFSA. Rules and regulations of the SFSA include both legally binding regulations and recommended guidelines issued by SFSA.

Prerequisites for Authorization

[244] Authorization for operations on the financial sector in Sweden is granted only when the entity applying for authorization meets the necessary regulatory requirements. The requirements generally include the following criteria, *inter alia* that:

(i) the company's articles of association, by-laws or regulations are in accordance with the provisions of the relevant governing act and otherwise contain the specific provisions required taking into consideration the scope and nature of the planned operations;
(ii) the company is managed in a professional manner and according to sound and prudent business principles;
(iii) the holder or anticipated holder of a qualified holding in the undertaking is deemed suitable to exercise a significant influence over the management of the company; and
(iv) it can be ascertained that the board of directors and the managing director possess sufficient insight and experience to participate in the management of the company.

[245] Detailed conditions governing the authorization for banking and financing businesses, fund management companies and payment service institutions are set out in the Banking and Financing Business Act, the Swedish UCITS Act, the Payment Services Act as well as the relevant government ordinances and SFSA rules, regulations and guidelines.

Application for Authorization

[246] The application for an operating authorization must be submitted to the SFSA, with supporting documents attached. Once the application has been filed, the SFSA must announce its decision within three months of receipt of the application, in regard to payment service institutions, or six months in regard to banking or financing business. However, this time limit provides that the application is accompanied by all the required information and that the relevant application fee is paid.

Notification of Acquisition of Ownership

[247] Any person or entity who contemplates acquiring a direct or indirect ownership of more than 10% of the voting rights in a credit institution or other SFSA supervised entity must submit a prior written notification to the SFSA. If the ownership is further increased to 20%, 30% or 50%, a new notification must be submitted prior to completion of the acquisition.

[248] In connection with the notification regarding the acquisition, the acquirer must also provide the SFSA with a so-called fit and proper notification regarding the reliability and eligibility of the shareholders. The evaluation is the same as is conducted concerning the management of the supervised entity. In evaluating the reliability and eligibility of the shareholders, the SFSA will assess, on the basis of the information received, the reliability, reputation, experience and eligibility of shareholder, and whether it can be ascertained that the organization will be managed in a professional manner and according to sound and prudent business principles.

Banking Operations by Foreign Entities

[249] A foreign entity which has been authorized in its home country in the EEA may provide financial services in Sweden either by establishing a branch office in Sweden or by providing cross-border services without establishing a physical presence in the country.

[250] In the event a branch office is established in Sweden by a credit institution, a financial institution or a fund management company, such branch office is subject to the SFSA receiving a prior notification to this effect from the home country supervisory authority if the home country is a Member State of the EEA. In case the credit institution, financial institution or the fund management company is authorized by a non-EEA country, the SFSA must first grant an authorization before such institution may provide financial services in Sweden. Such authorization shall be granted where:

(i) the institution is subject to satisfactory supervision by a competent authority in the home state and the authority has consented to the undertaking establishing itself in Sweden;
(ii) there is reason to assume that the planned operations will be conducted in a manner which is compatible with the requirements in the Banking and Financing Business Act; and
(iii) deposits with the branch are covered by a guarantee in accordance with the Deposits Guarantee Act (1995:1571, as amended) or by a foreign guarantee which corresponds to the guarantee stated in the Deposits Guarantee Act.

[251] In case no branch office is established, a credit institution, financial institution or a fund management company authorized in an EEA country may provide cross-border services by notifying the relevant authorities. Services can be offered when the SFSA has received a notification of the provision of services from the supervisory authority of the home country. The notification shall contain a description of the types of services that the foreign institution intends to offer in Sweden.

Insurance Companies

[252] In Sweden, the conduct of insurance business is subject to obtaining a licence from the SFSA, which grants licences for insurance companies, mutual insurance companies, insurance associations as well as insurance companies from outside the EEA. The insurance sector is supervised by the SFSA, which is the national authority for supervision of Sweden's financial and insurance sectors. The objective of the SFSA is to ensure financial stability and balanced operations of regulated insurance companies and to safeguard the interests of the insured.

[253] Insurance legislation in Sweden contains separate laws on, *inter alia*, insurance companies, foreign insurance companies and insurance contracts and is based mostly on EU directives. The Swedish legislation in the insurance sector is harmonized with the EU legislation. The main legislation in the insurance sector includes the Insurance Business Act (2010:2043, as amended), the Insurance Contracts Act (2005:104, as amended) and the Insurance Mediation Act (2018:1219, as amended).

[254] Besides the SFSA, other authorities and organizations are responsible for different parts of the insurance sector. The Swedish Social Insurance Agency (Sw. *Försäkringskassan*) is responsible for administering social insurance benefits with regards to, *inter alia*, illness, disability and families with children. In addition, the Swedish Pensions Agency (Sw. *Pensionsmyndigheten*) is responsible for the national public pension.

2.3.2 Energy Market

[255] The main legislation in the energy market sector includes the Electricity Act (1997:857, as amended) and the Natural Gas Act (2005:403, as amended). The Swedish Energy Markets Inspectorate (Sw. *Energimarknadsinspektionen*) (the 'Ei') is the national regulatory authority for electricity and natural gas markets. The principal task of the Ei is to regulate the pricing and the terms of transmission, distribution and other network services in both the electricity and the natural gas markets. Both the electricity and natural gas network operations are subject to licence in the form of concession granted by the Ei.

3 ANTITRUST/COMPETITION ISSUES

3.1 Legislation and Competent Authorities

[256] The principal law concerning competition issues in Sweden is the Competition Act (2008:579, as amended, Sw. *Konkurrenslagen*). The Competition Act rests upon three central provisions: prohibition of anticompetitive agreements and cooperation between companies, prohibition of abuse of dominance and merger control. Swedish competition law is principally harmonized with EU competition rules, in terms of both language and interpretation of the rules. EU competition issues are regulated pursuant to Articles 101–109 of the Treaty on the Functioning of the European Union (TFEU), which include provisions on state aid, as well as through a series of regulations and directives derived thereby.

[257] The Swedish Competition Authority (Sw. *Konkurrensverket*) is a public supervisory authority in the field of competition law. The main task of the Swedish Competition Authority is to safeguard and increase competition and supervise public procurement in Sweden to the benefit of consumers. It also has the right to intervene, where necessary, in restrictive practices, such as cartels and abuse of dominant position, violating the Competition Act and Articles 101 and 102 TFEU, which form the basis of competition policy. The EU competition rules are applicable in cases where trade between Member States may be affected. The Swedish Competition Act is applicable if a restriction on competition has effects on trade within Sweden. Where trade between Member States may also be affected, the EU competition rules apply in parallel with Swedish law. For example, an agreement between companies operating only on the Swedish market can hinder imports and thus affect trade between Member States. Competition restrictions are investigated both on the Swedish Competition Authority's own initiative, on the basis of complaints received from third parties, and as a result of a leniency application where a company discloses its participation in an illegal anticompetitive cooperation such as a cartel.

[258] As of writing, the Swedish Competition Authority is still one of the few competition authorities in the EU that lacks its own decision-making powers in the enforcement of the competition rules. Under the current framework, a judicial model applies where the Swedish Competition Authority must bring an action in the Patent and Market Court to impose fines on companies for violating the competition rules. The decision of the Patent and Market Court can be appealed to the Patent and Market Court of Appeal, which, as a general rule, is the highest judicial body resolving upon competition issues. The penalty payment may also be imposed on an undertaking or an association of undertakings to whom the business activity involved in the infringement has been transferred as a result of a concentration or other corporate transaction. In 2020 the Swedish Government proposed granting the Competition Authority greater decision-making powers including for competition fines and investigative fines.

3.2 Merger Control

[259] The Swedish merger control provisions in Chapter 4 of the Competition Act apply to transactions that meet the national thresholds. Transactions which fall within the scope of the EU Merger Regulation (Council Regulation (EC) No. 139/2004 on the control of concentrations between undertakings (as amended)) shall be notified to the European Commission.

[260] Transactions exceeding the turnover thresholds as specified in Chapter 4, section 6 in the Competition Act must be notified to the Swedish Competition Authority and the transaction must not be implemented prior to the Swedish Competition Authority's approval of the transaction. In its assessment, the Competition Authority will consider if the transaction is liable to significantly impede the existence or development of effective competition in the relevant markets. Most transactions do not raise competition concerns and therefore can be completed without further measures. By contrast, transactions raising material competition concerns will not be authorized by competition authorities without adequate commitments by the parties aimed at addressing those concerns. This means that the parties will offer and be required to either divest an undertaking, or a part of a business (so-called structural remedies) or take other measures that will have a favourable effect on competition, for example access to key technology, supply and licensing (so-called behavioural remedies).

[261] If a satisfactory conclusion cannot be obtained by imposing commitments and the transaction will unavoidably significantly impede the existence or development of effective competition on the whole, or a substantial part, of the Swedish market, the transaction will be prohibited. However, prohibition decisions issued by the Swedish Competition Authority against mergers are uncommon.

[262] As of 2018, the Swedish Competition Authority has the power to make decisions on prohibition mergers without having to bring an action in court. Moreover, in 2018, the Swedish Competition Authority issued Guidelines on Merger Control (617/2017) (*Konkurrensverkets vägledning för anmälan och prövning av företagskoncentrationer*). The objective of the Guidelines on Merger Control is to clarify the principles adhered to in the interpretation of the provisions on merger control and to provide more detailed instructions on the application of the provisions. The Guidelines on Merger Control deal with issues such as the notification obligation and procedure, the EU-dimension and the assessment of mergers.

3.2.1 Scope of Application

[263] Pursuant to Chapter 4 of the Competition Act, a concentration must be notified to the Swedish Competition Authority if the combined Swedish turnover of the parties to the concentration exceeds SEK1 billion and the individual Swedish turnover of at least two of the parties exceeds SEK200 million.

[264] In the context of the Swedish merger control rules, a concentration shall be deemed to arise where control of the undertakings has permanently changed as a result of:

(i) the merger of two or more previously independent undertakings; or
(ii) the acquisition through the purchase of shares or assets, by agreement or otherwise, of direct or indirect control of one or more undertakings or parts thereof by one or more persons who already control at least one undertaking, or by one or more undertakings.

Similar to the EU Merger Regulation, the provisions on the control of concentrations shall not apply to internal arrangements within a group of companies.

[265] Moreover, as stated above, the provisions of the Competition Act concerning merger control do not apply if the concentration falls within the scope of the EU Merger Regulation. The European Commission has the sole right to examine concentrations having a community dimension. However, the European Commission has the power to refer a concentration to the Swedish Competition Authority (or any other national competition authority in the EU).

3.2.2 Assessment of Concentrations

[266] In its assessment of concentrations, the Swedish Competition Authority uses a competition test that corresponds to the so-called SIEC test of the EC Merger Regulation. Pursuant to the competition test, the Swedish Competition Authority intervenes with a concentration if, as a result of it, the concentration may significantly impede effective competition in the Swedish markets or a substantial part thereof, in particular as a result of the creation or strengthening of a dominant position. From the perspective of the appraisal process, the test is designed specifically to measure how much competition is lost as a result of the merger. The future development of the markets is also sought to be taken into consideration as well as the views of the main competitors to the parties to the concentration, customers and suppliers alike.

3.2.3 Notification Procedure and Timing

[267] A merger notification to the Swedish Competition Authority is a fairly straightforward process where the Competition Authority generally is willing to engage in a proactive dialogue in order to reach an approval of the transaction. Prior to the submission of the filing, the parties of the concentration may request a preliminary meeting with the Competition Authority to discuss the planned transaction and raise potential concerns regarding market definitions. In addition, the parties may request advice in relation to the documents to be provided and some particular questions of the case that are of interest to the Swedish Competition Authority. Such preliminary discussions are not mandatory but may facilitate drafting the notification and serve to help the Swedish Competition Authority to process the matter quickly.

[268] Pursuant to the Competition Act, the acquiring party has the obligation to notify the transaction. If the transaction concerns a joint venture, the parties forming the joint venture have a joint obligation to notify the transaction.

[269] Under the Competition Act, there is no fixed deadline within which the concentration should be notified to the Swedish Competition Authority. Instead, a concentration may be notified to the Swedish Competition Authority as soon as a party or any other participant can show that they intend to carry out a concentration between undertakings, and must be made before the concentration between undertakings is carried out. The notification shall be completed in accordance with the detailed instructions set out in the Swedish Competition Authority's regulations and instructions for notification of company concentration (KKVFS 2010:3). The regulation also lists the information to be provided in the notification.

[270] After the notification has been submitted, the Swedish Competition Authority has twenty-five business days to decide whether to clear the transaction (phase 1) or to open an in-depth investigation of the transaction (phase 2). In case the Swedish Competition Authority does not decide to open a phase 2 investigation regarding the transaction, the transaction is considered to be approved. In regards to a phase 2 investigation, the Swedish Competition Authority has a period of three months to investigate the transaction further. Within this three-month period, the Competition Authority must either approve the transaction, with or without conditions, or issue a prohibition of the transaction.

[271] The parties to the concentration cannot take measures to implement the concentration before the Competition Authority has given its final approval without conditions, or with conditions attached (so-called standstill obligation). According to the Swedish Competition Authority's Guidelines on Merger Control (617/2017), this standstill obligation also applies to acquisition of securities traded on a stock exchange. However, the parties to the concentration may request the Swedish Competition Authority to grant an exemption permission to implement the transaction prior to its final approval.

3.2.4 Sanctions

[272] As mentioned above, the parties to the concentration cannot implement or take any actions to implement the transaction prior to its approval by the Swedish Competition Authority. Any breach of the obligation not to implement the transaction prior to it being approved (so-called gun-jumping) may result in penalty payments (fines) being imposed. The Swedish Competition Authority decides upon the penalty payment and its amount, which will be based on an overall assessment. In practice, the penalty payments have ranged between SEK10 million and 100 million.

4 EMPLOYMENT CONSIDERATIONS

4.1 Regulatory Framework

4.1.1 Employment Protection Act and Other Applicable Laws

[273] The Swedish labour market system is regulated by employment law and collective bargaining agreements. The labour market in Sweden is to a great extent self-regulated by employers' organizations and trade unions. Mandatory laws and regulations in collective bargaining agreements provide a comprehensive framework for the terms and conditions of employment. Collective bargaining agreements are of great importance, and they often contain regulations deviating from statutory provisions to better suit the type of business where they apply. For example, there are no provisions regarding minimum salary in Swedish labour law. However, provisions regarding such matters are often found in the collective bargaining agreements.

[274] The Employment Protection Act (1982:80, as amended) is the main statute applicable to employment relationships. The Employment Protection Act applies to employees in the public or private sectors, except for:

(i) employees who hold a senior management or comparable position;

(ii) employees who are members of the employer's family;
(iii) employees who are employed for work in the employer's household;
(iv) employees who are employed with a special recruitment incentive, in sheltered employment, or with a wage subsidy for development in employment; and
(v) employees who are employed in an upper secondary school apprenticeship.

The Employment Protection Act sets out, among other things, general rules and regulations, employees' and employers' obligations and the process of terminating employments.

[275] Other relevant laws are *inter alia* the Employment (Co-determination in the Workplace) Act (1976:580, as amended), the Annual Leave Act (1977:480, as amended), the Working Hours Act (1982:673, as amended), the Public Employment Act (1994:260, as amended), the Anti-Discrimination Act (2008:567, as amended) and the Work Environment Act (1977:1160, as amended).

4.1.2 Collective Bargaining Agreements

[276] Collective bargaining agreements are agreements between employer and employee associations. They are usually industry-wide and define the minimum rights and obligations of the employer and the employees during the agreement period, which is usually a fixed term of one to three years. Collective bargaining agreements largely determine the contents of employment relationship, such as wages, benefits, holidays and working hours. In the Swedish labour market collective bargaining takes place at three levels: (i) between employers' associations and nationwide trade unions on national level, (ii) between the individual unions and employers' industry associations at industry-wide or branch level and (iii) between the employer and the local union at local level.

[277] During the term of the collective bargaining agreement, industrial actions (strikes), the right to which is generally guaranteed by the Constitution, are prohibited. Striking is permitted after an agreement has ended, and if the strike is lawful, employees are protected against dismissal and claims for damages.

4.1.3 Act on Cooperation Within Undertakings

[278] The Employment (Co-determination in the Workplace) Act applies to the relationship between employers and employees. In the Act, the term employee shall also include any person who performs work for another and is not thereby employed by that other person but who has a position which is substantially similar to that of an employee. The Employment (Co-determination in the Workplace) Act sets out provisions regarding the right for employees to exercise influence over matters relating to the work, working conditions and position of the employees in the company, such as the right of association and the right of negotiation. In addition to the Employment (Co-determination in the Workplace) Act, the provisions in the collective bargaining agreements need to be taken into consideration in matters within the scope of the Cooperation Act.

4.2 Employment Protection and Benefits

4.2.1 Employment Protection

[279] The Employment Protection Act and the applicable collective bargaining agreement set out the minimum terms for the employment contract between the employer and the employee. The employer and the employee may always agree on terms that are more favourable for the employee.

[280] Based on its right of direction and supervision, the employer may unilaterally decide on certain changes to the work and working conditions of the employee. Such changes, however, cannot amend the terms of the employment contract. Any amendment to the employment contract needs to be mutually agreed upon between the employer and the employee. If such mutual agreement cannot be reached, the amendment may only be implemented by terminating the employment contract, provided that applicable grounds for termination exist.

[281] The employer and the employee can freely agree on the minimum duration of the employment relationship agreement provided that the contract is reasonable. However, a general fixed-term employment becomes employment for an indefinite term when an employee has been employed by the employer for general fixed-term employment for an aggregate period of more than two years during a five-year period.

[282] Depending on the size of the company, the members of the company's management, excluding the managing director, may be considered to be employees of the company and thus be covered by the employment law. However, there are certain exceptions which concern the management. For example, the Working Hours Act is not applicable to work performed by employees who, taking into consideration their duties and terms and conditions of employment, hold a senior management or comparable positions or by employees who, taking into consideration their duties, are entrusted with arranging their own working hours. Further, it is customary that the management is excluded from the scope of applicability of collective bargaining agreements.

[283] Under Swedish employment law, a managing director is not considered an employee but a separate corporate organ (similar to the board of directors), and therefore neither the collective bargaining agreements nor the Swedish employment protection act applies to the managing director, unless otherwise agreed.

4.2.2 Agreement of Non-competition or Non-solicitation

[284] An agreement made at the beginning of, or during the employment relationship, may limit the employee's right to conclude an employment contract with a competing firm and also the employee's right to engage in competing operations on his or her own account (agreement of non-competition). Agreements of non-competition are not governed by the Employment Protection Act, but rather by the Contracts Act section 38, which allows such agreements provided that the agreement is reasonable. To the extent that the agreement of non-competition goes beyond the allowed restrictions set out in the Contracts Act, such agreement will be invalid. According to collective bargaining agreements and case law, the period of a non-compete covenant should generally not exceed nine months following termination of employment, and should only in exceptional circumstances exceed eighteen months.

[285] The employer and the employee can also agree on confidentiality or that the employee is not allowed to entice away from the employer any employee of the company for a certain period of time (agreement of non-solicitation). The agreement may include a provision on contractual penalty. The Labour Court has found that there are reasons to be restrictive when it comes to allowing non-solicitation clauses. The restrictive period cannot go beyond what is considered reasonable and the employer must have a legitimate interest. In a case from 2018, the Labour Court found that a period of six months' non-solicitation post-termination was unreasonable.

4.2.3 Pension Arrangements and Social Security

[286] In Sweden, all employers are obliged to pay certain insurance and social security contributions. Persons working in the private sector are insured in accordance with the Social Insurance Code (2010:110, as amended) irrespective of an employee's field of work, earnings or length of contract.

[287] The Swedish pension system consists of three parts: a national public pension from the state, occupational pension from the employer and any personal savings. The national public pension is based on the person's income through life and is administered and paid by the Swedish Pensions Agency. It is not mandatory for employers to offer occupational pension. Nevertheless, occupational pension is offered to all governmental employees and most of the employees in the private sector, especially those covered by a collective bargaining agreement. The employer can choose the pension insurance company in which it insures its employees. The employment pension contributions are formed in every pension company on similar grounds, based on the employee's salary.

[288] Furthermore, the employer is obliged to pay mandatory contributions with respect to its employees such as, *inter alia*: (i) social security contributions to be paid to the tax authorities; (ii) accident insurance premium, the amount of which varies according to the sector or industry; and (iii) sickness benefit premium. Generally, a Swedish employer has to insure a foreign employee working in Sweden in the same way as Swedish employees.

4.3 Transfer of Employees in Business Transfer

4.3.1 Principle of Continuity

[289] A sale of shares does not, as such, affect the employment agreement between the employer and the employee. According to the Employment Protection Act, neither will a whole or partial sale of the business affect the employment relationship, as the employment relationship will be automatically transferred to the acquirer in connection with a business transfer. However, the employment agreement and the employment relationship may not be transferred to a new employer where the employee objects thereto. The transfer also includes employment-related rights, obligations and benefits under the relevant employment relationships. This means that the employees will transfer as 'old employees' and the employment relationships continue without any interruption. Unless the parties to the transfer agree otherwise, the transferor is liable to compensate such claims pertaining to the time before the transfer to the transferee. Further, pursuant to the Employment Protection Act, a transfer of business is not, as such, a legal and sufficient ground to terminate any employment relationship.

4.3.2 Right of Negotiation

[290] The Employment (Co-determination in the Workplace) Act provides that prior to making a decision regarding a material change in its business activities, such as a business transfer, an employer shall, on his own initiative, negotiate with the employee organization to which he is bound by a collective bargaining agreement. This obligation for the employer to negotiate also applies to employee organizations to which the employer is not bound by a collective agreement if the matter specifically relates to the working conditions or employment terms and conditions of an employee who belongs to such an employee organization.

4.3.3 Collective Bargaining Agreements

[291] Where a business is transferred from an employer who is bound by a collective bargaining agreement to a new employer, the agreement shall apply, in pertinent part, to the new employer. However, the collective bargaining agreement shall not apply where the new employer is already bound by another collective agreement which may be applied to the employees included in the transfer. The employee may give notice of termination of the collective bargaining agreement within thirty days after it has been informed of the transfer. In that case, the agreement shall terminate at the time of the transfer or, where notice of termination is given after the transfer, at the time that notice is given.

5 ACCOUNTING TREATMENT IN SWEDEN

[292] Swedish publicly listed companies prepare their group accounts, with regards to the format and content, in accordance with IFRS as adopted by the EU together with International Accounting Standards (IAS). Use of IFRS is permitted for unlisted domestic companies in both consolidated and separate company statements.

5.1 Accounting Treatment for Business Combinations

[293] IFRS is applied for business combinations; i.e., companies may not adopt different merger and acquisition accounting, nor adopt various accounting treatments. Business combinations are treated in accordance with the amended IFRS 3 – 'Business Combinations', which applies the acquisition method to business combinations, the amended IAS 27 – 'Separate Financial Statements' and the amended IFRS 10 – 'Consolidated Financial Statements'. Under IFRS, all combinations are acquisitions, and contingent purchase price is valued at fair value. Any subsequent changes in the purchase price will be to the statement of income, rather than by adjusting goodwill. Additionally, expenses relating to the acquisition are not capitalized but recognized directly onto the statement of income as an expense (e.g., for legal and other services rendered).

5.2 Accounting Treatment of Goodwill

[294] In accordance with the acquisition method, the amount of goodwill arising from the combination is recognized and may not be amortized. Instead of being amortized, goodwill is tested for impairment on a yearly basis (or more often if there is a triggering event). Additionally, impairment charges may not be reversed and negative goodwill is recognized immediately in accordance with IFRS (the amended IAS 36 – 'Impairment of Assets'). The test for impairment is performed in connection with the test of the 'Cash Generating Unit' by applying the bottom-up/top-down method where the book value of goodwill is allocated to the cash flow producing unit.

5.3 Accounting Treatment of Intangible Assets

[295] IFRS standards derive the definition of intangible assets from the IAS standards (the amended IAS 38 – 'Intangible Assets'). IAS 38 requires an entity to recognize an intangible asset if, and only if, it is identifiable and specific criteria are met. An identifiable intangible asset is separable and arises from contractual or other legal rights. The intangible asset must additionally be controllable by the acquirer and the asset must provide an expected financial gain. IAS 38 further specifies how to measure the carrying amount of intangible assets and requires specified disclosures regarding intangible assets. In addition to IAS 38, IFRS 3 also includes a list of intangible assets that satisfy the criteria of being recognized apart from goodwill, e.g. brands and licences. Intangible assets having an indefinite useful life are recognized separately from goodwill and may not be amortized.

www.ingramcontent.com/pod-product-compliance
Lightning Source LLC
Chambersburg PA
CBHW071359230926
51846CB00002B/599
9789403531601